To Ken
With Best Wishes -
for purchasing the book.

Leaving the Past Behind
By Norman Williams

First published in 2019

ISBN: 9781081110864

Norman Williams

Forward

I first met Norman in the village hall at Acton Trussell where we used to take my late father-in-law for his weekly coffee morning outing. On this particular day there was quite a buzz about the place which on further investigation turned out to be Norman, in full flow, reminiscing on his childhood and other stories.

Norman had found the hall quite by chance having been passing and had dropped in to have a quick brew. A natural and engaging storyteller, it didn't take long before he became the centre of attention with a wide circle of listeners enthralled by his adventures. Norman went on to become a regular at the weekly gathering and, one day, I heard someone suggest he should write his stories down so they could be heard by a wider audience - 'I have!' said Norman gleefully, 'I have them on my word-processor at home although I don't know how anyone would see them...'

This gave me the idea to see if I could bring them to light and the result is what you have in your hands!

It has taken some time and a lot of help from Lin and Mel from Staffordshire Publishers to get the manuscript into a publishable state. I am grateful for the many hours they have put in and to those who have also contributed.

Norman has asked for any profit that the book may make be donated to local military charities, so you will forgive me for asking you to spread the word and help make it the best seller it deserves to be!

Finally, thank you for picking this up. I hope you enjoy and value reading it as much as we have in publishing it.

Martin White
August 2019

To the Reader

To the reader of these memoirs, I would just like to say they are not in any way a literary accomplishment, but are more likely a diary of events, happenings and memories, that in writing have helped me in some way towards living.

I would ask you to criticise viciously rather than gently. I often believe there is more to be learnt by knowing the bad points, rather than the good. In most cases the good points look after themselves.

If you know me, then I hope it will not affect your feelings in a downward trend, thus diluting much of what you may have valued.

These memoirs must do for me, now. I dare say I will think of something that I've forgotten and might well be worth recording. After all you can't write everything that's happened in a lifetime, that can be read in something like eight or ten hours and in the time it's taken to write, recall everything that's happened in that lifetime.

My thanks to you for taking the time to read them.

Norman

Leaving the Past Behind

Preface

The real purpose for writing these memoirs is for me. To restrict and deter and abolish if possible, the abysmal feelings that have monopolised me since the first of April 2010, when I lost my dear wife Freda. To get rid of the misery that tends to breed, develop and multiply with every day that passes, which is only curbed by the fact I have children and are surrounded broadly speaking by lovely people, otherwise life wouldn't be worth a light.

I suppose I must add that one or two have said I must write a diary, a book, or keep a record but I believe these suggestions were fostered by snippets of my army life which some found of interest. On giving much thought to this and remembering the wonderful people I've met in my life I've decided to give it a go.

Another reason, especially for my children, is to supply answers to the questions they nearly always think of when it is too late. This is a common occurrence. How I wished I'd asked more, listened more and thought more of those who were the informants.

Although these memoirs are memories, don't think for a moment you can learn everything about a person's life in a few hours of reading, when it took something like ninety years to happen and these ninety years when young, seemed for ever, far into the distance, but now that it is here, is merely a momentum. Such is life.

In doing so I am sure that much of what I write will be, to the reader, of small worth, perhaps trivial and inconsequential, but nevertheless it will be written because of its worth and the value to me of the people I've known.

Now to the acknowledgements, credits, call them what you will. To me they are more like a Roll of Honour. First and foremost, Freda my wife, to whom I owe so much, her love, our happiness and our children and figures so greatly in my life.

Then there are our children, Melanie and Glen, who as children brought us much joy and as adults have added to that joy many times over.

Then strangely enough there are three women, three ladies by the names of Maureen, Jean and Audrey who I will always be grateful to, for knowing, though it was only for a very short time.

Then there are family relatives, none on my side now, but those on Freda's who it is always a privilege, a pleasure and a joy to meet, though sadly, usually only about once per year. I'm not going to mention names they all know who they are but may not know how valuable they are to me and were to Freda.

And now the everyday wonderful folk, living close by in some cases, serving in supermarkets, shops, offices or factories or retired, citizens of the village, all of supreme value. These citizens, all of these people are truly part of the richness of life. Now to the beginning.

In October 2016, I was invited by the Royal British Legion to visit Normandy, but in doing so it was necessary for me to leave my car somewhere close to the station, to avoid walking, especially with carrying a suitcase. The nearest street, where parking was for residents only. I knocked on the door of the first house, and a young lady about late thirties came to the door and immediately said there is a parking space in the private apartment block opposite where her friend lived, and she could arrange for me to use it. In a second she was on the phone and almost immediately the friend came over, all smiles and agreed, but then the young lady said. "No, I'll park my car there and you can use my space in front of the house. It will be easier for you."

I returned to park my car at 5 o'clock as agreed, to leave it for five days. Again, she spotted me and came out, this time with her delightful children, one, a little boy, stood before me like a little man and he addressed me so intelligently, so politely by asking "What is your name?" and I replied "Norman Williams." He studied me for a moment and then said, "Norman can you take me to the park?" It maybe doesn't read with much importance, but I nearly melted. It felt more like an accolade and then the mother said some kindly words and led me to her car, the children jumping inside as well, and she ran me to the station. At the station she carried my bag and led me to a bench seat on the correct platform. Thinking she had left and seeing an earlier train on the illuminated sign, I ventured into the hall to check the trains, when from nowhere she appeared, informing me that when my train arrived, one of the station staff would come and help me and guide me to my seat. All this was done for me by this lady and I don't even know her name, but she lives on in my memory.

Then there are others near-by where I live, Carol who with her five friends, including her husband Steve, presented me with a birthday card, followed by numerous presents of all kinds of eatables at a Live and Local show at the village hall. I was dumbfounded and I can still hardly believe it. All because in booking my tickets with her, I happened to mention "Oh! It's on my birthday." From that remark they arranged, that delightful, totally unexpected surprise and they are now firm friends of mine. I can't believe how lucky I am!

Now another. It's July 2017 and I contacted a company in Cheshire, the lady in question, who told me the price of the items I wanted. It was hugely increased from my last dealings in 2005. Then she asked me how much I wanted, and she said. "Give me a day or two and I'll ring you back." This happened and when I asked her "How much?" She replied. "Oh! It's nothing." Believe me the amount was substantial and here she was giving it me for nothing and what is more, like the first contact with the lady at the village hall mentioned above, she was waiting for my arrival and came out of her office, the moment I stepped out of my car. This tells me so much of the quality and kindness of these people, much more than words can say.

I can't quite understand how fortunate I am. A retired Police Inspector, only this morning has cut the top and the neighbour's side of the six-foot-high hedge that runs the width of my lawn. Yesterday, he said, as I was cutting the front of the hedge. "Don't you go getting up ladders. I'll do it in the morning." Morning came and looking out of my bedroom window I discovered it was done. He must have cut it just after he spoke about it, whilst I was out. This is a man who has done so much for one and the other. There could be a lot more which I don't know about and as it's unlikely that rewards, or mention, or even thought, may be given to him, I, at least feel better that I have written these few words about him.

Now to John, Gwilliam Jones, a teacher who opened my eyes to the beauty of the English language, Literature and Drama.

My wife who was part of me for sixty years and was taken away from me nine long years ago.

Our two children, Melanie and Glen. "What can I say?"

My family have furnished, provided and sustained the whole of my life.

2019.

Leaving the Past Behind

Chapter 1

A Boy

But first as I've said, it has been suggested to me on several occasions by different people that I should write a record of things that have happened to me or I have experienced and I suppose now in my early nineties it is time I did so if ever I'm going to. Mind you, I think most of the reasoning is related to my army life, which seems to be of more interest to most people than the rest of it, but to please myself, I intend to start at the beginning and to work right through, bringing to mind the many incredible personages, many of them quite wonderful people who have crossed my path in life and indeed should be remembered and will be.

I feel I must hurry because life is on the move, shooting by, very, very, fast and with it comes the memory fade and the unbearable thought that I may not be able to remember all that I would wish to. Already I feel I may have lost some valuable memories and for this reason if for no other, this record may be sketchy and out of line with regard to continuity. That being so, the date and place of my birth might be a good starting point.

I was born on the fourth of March 1925 in Greenbank Buildings, Upton, Wirral, Merseyside. I have no memory of that location. My earliest memories are of Greasby, a village a mile or so from Upton, towards Frankby.

We, my mother, brothers George and Sam lived in a wooden typed bungalow which I believe my father largely built himself. Heating was an open coal fire; lighting was by oil lamps. We had no gas or electricity. The toilet was in a hut up the garden. Attached to the bungalow at the side was a barn-like structure. Dolly, (half horse and half mule) lived in the barn which had a boarded space above which stored the hay for her bedding and her feed.

On a memorable occasion my brother George, some years older than me was lighting matches and spinning them between finger and thumb creating a whirring sound with a comet-like trail as it spun through the air. One of the spins soared upwards and set alight to the hay. In no time at all the building was ablaze. The fire engine was called, and I can remember walking amongst the firemen and the neighbouring onlookers with my blonde head of curls and winning from the assembly quite an amount of pennies and halfpennies. George meanwhile had disappeared and was nowhere to be seen. He was found later hiding under the double bed in my parent's bedroom. I remember my mother, her face wan and pale looking extremely worried and frail. I've got a feeling she'd been ill, maybe it was the rheumatic fever which I know she did have whilst at Greasby and she had to be isolated in the old fever hospital due to the severity of the illness.

George seemed to be obsessed by fire. On an earlier occasion before I was born, he was in bed and was striking matches and dropping them all around him, fortunately Sammy who was always mature and like a little adult with a certain amount of nosiness or authority, looked in, saw and raised the alarm. My father grabbed the baby then threw the burning mattress through the window onto the ground below and George escaped unharmed. It was oil lamps and candles that were used extensively as a means of lighting so matches were nearly always to hand and consequently could be an ever-present risk.

I remember also at about two years of age being ill with double pneumonia and my mother constantly at my bedside waiting for the fever to break or as they said in those days for the crisis to be reached and then later when I was recovering, watching my mother playing cricket with the boys outside at the back of the house. My mother having placed the bed near the window so that I could see her and by seeing her, be reassured of her presence.

The bungalow we lived in had no gas or electricity, the only means of heating was by the coal fire in the living room and by stone hot water bottles in the bedroom. My most vivid memory of those days was in the winter, sitting before the flickering coal fire, in the lamp light, rubbing my feet with one of those spiky pin-like hairbrushes in an endeavour to ease the pain and itching of chilblains in my frozen feet.

My earliest recollection of friends at this time was what they call a spirit friend named Badock. This was a friend apparently that was seen by me but seemingly by no one else. I used to share sweets with him and make sure a place was there for him to sit down. It is said by Spiritualists that these friends are sent down as company for children who are alone and live perhaps in isolated places. I was suitable I guess because there were no other small children about when I was that age.

I also remember in this period after terrible wet and windy weather finding at the edge of the brook which ran at the end of our road and which gave its name to Brookdale Avenue, a green pound note. My mother said I knew what it was because I'd seen the letters written by my father from Llandudno and often contained such a note or perhaps more than one, as he sent money to my mother. As an example of the honesty of the age and in particular my mother, she gently washed the note, ironed it and retained it until the following week when the Co-op baker, who as he delivered, mentioned his bad luck the previous week, when he was short by one pound on his bread round, which he must have dropped in the area and found its way to the muddy banks of the brook where I was destined to find it. On hearing the story from my mother and receiving the pound note he was overjoyed and immediately stuck his hand into his pocket and withdrew half a crown and insisted on my mother accepting it. When I tell you the man's wages in those days was little over a pound you can understand his initial despair and later his jubilation and his generosity. I believe it was on that occasion I was insisting on telling the Co-op man by persistently pulling at his trouser leg, pointing at our black and white kitten and repeatedly saying "Look he's got a little white belly." All this despite my mother's quiet tapping at me to keep quiet, but it was not to be, until finally he looked, slightly embarrassed, even blushing and said, "Oh yes," that I was satisfied. People seemed to be far more sensitive about things in those days than what they are today.

Another memory is the World Jamboree held at Arrowe Park near Birkenhead, but nearer to Greasby, in 1929, the year of the great American financial crash, during the most torrential weather and on the last night in the presence of Lord Baden Powell, the Chief Scout and scouts from every corner of the world; they held a magnificent enormous firework display. I can still remember vividly sitting astride my Brother Sam's shoulders as he jumped over the water and mud filled ditches and then witnessed goggle eyed the array of light, sparks, explosions and awesome display. I still consider it the greatest of firework displays, but obviously this opinion is coloured by memory, the passing of time and my years of immaturity.

I also remember my mother one dark winter's night in the early evening buying a goat-chair, the modern version being a push chair. I can see her now looking at it outside the shop, on display under the old-fashioned glass veranda, a price tag on it 3/6 or 7/- I can't remember which. My mother spoke to the man in the shop, emptied her purse, returned outside, sat me in it and off we went.

At the time she was making a set of loose covers for some people who lived in Moreton. My mother pushed me all the way in the goat-chair (I think that was the main reason she bought it). We were shown into a cold bare room, pale green in colour, with just the furniture that needed the covers in front of us. My mother had to fit them, then unpick and re-sew by hand the offending parts until it was skin-tight, no fullness, no creases, just perfect. We were there 'til 9 or 10 o'clock and then had to walk back all the way home, several miles. I can still hear my mother murmuring in slightly disgruntled tones - "All that time and not even a cup of tea." Such was the courage, tenacity and the ability to work virtually all hours, that was certainly my mother's forte and probably many other women's too, but more about my mother later.

At this time my father had left Greasby and was living and working in Llandudno.

In 1930 when I was five my mother and my brother George and I moved to Llandudno to join my father. My brother Sam stopped in Greasby and lived with a couple who lived in Brookdale Avenue. The principal reason being that he was apprenticed to Atkinson's the builders and in those days if you had a job you made certain you kept it.

We were taken from Greasby in a coal wagon owned by my mother's brother, Foster. At Craigside near the Little Orme end of Llandudno we all had to get out to push the vehicle up the hill. In those days a tram track ran alongside and in the Summer months it was a lovely ride on what they called the Toast Track which was in effect a roofless open tram and it ran from West Shore in Llandudno through the fields at Craig-y-Don past the rear of the

Little Orme and on to Colwyn Bay a distance of about six or seven miles.

At Llandudno we lived in a bottom flat at a house right on the sea front at the Parade at Craig-y-Don. The house was called "Kestin." It's still there today under the same name.   It was owned by a woman of some fifty odd years who I remember mostly because she bathed in the sea all the year round. In the summer she would take my mother and our terrier (Spot the biter) and her dog, a spaniel, to the West Shore beach where they paddled in the shallow water, the dogs reluctantly swimming behind.

Spot the biter or Spot the fighter was a fox terrier who was fearless and was a character all on his own. Average size, smooth haired but knew no master, always challenging other dogs who when they retreated, left them alone, but if challenged fought and won, every time. The same with humans was independent and always warned you by wrinkling his nose, and then if you persisted, the next move was a bite. He was a total loner. Each  day he had his port of call which took him all over Llandudno. First to Billington and Brown the grocers on the corner of Queens Road and Victoria Street, for his morning currant bun, then to Nixon's sweet shop on the other corner of Victoria Street for his biscuit, then to Owens the butchers on the high street for his bone.

One day in this butcher's shop, sawdust wooden floor, the butcher threw a bone to Spot which skidded on the wooden floor and was seized by an Alsatian which was one of three who were owned by the same person. Spot immediately launched himself at the dog.

The man and the Alsatian beat a hasty retreat and the butcher threw a large bone to Spot saying "Good on yer" which Spot accepted, returned home with it and stored it in his kennel with no one able to touch it until he was out on his port of calls, then mother whilst he was absent would clean out his kennel. It was the only time it could be done. This same dog was responsible for my mother receiving several gifts which if couldn't be eaten would always be brought home, they included a fresh pound of best butter unopened (which was a prize in itself - few people could afford real butter in those days) and the finest pair of kid gloves my mother ever had, they were beautifully made and had two perfectly formed acorns featured on the wrists of each glove.

I remember him with a bar of chocolate placed between his front paws expertly opening it by the use of his teeth and paws. If my mother had to go anywhere, she was ever watchful that Spot was not around because if he was, he would follow her, hiding himself until the last moment then racing like mad to board the tram or bus my mother was getting on. My mother would immediately implore the conductor not to do anything with the dog (knowing he was likely to be bitten if he did) resulting in her getting off the vehicle with Spot following.

Another time a young man who made up bundles of firewood and sold them for a copper or two, called on people, hoping that they would purchase them. On this occasion for some reason the front door must have been partly open when he rang the bell. Spot shot down the hall, through the door and unknown to us, he bit the young man's hand.

Later that day at teatime the bell rang, and the young man was at the door. My father was at home, and on answering the door was presented with a hugely swollen hand and a gaping savage bite between finger and thumb. The young man said, "Have you got a bit of bandage?" "How did that happen?" my father countered. When he heard the story he took him in, bathed the wound with

Boracic powder in the water, put a dressing on with the special ointment (Zinc, Boracic and Vaseline in equal parts, you'll know about this eventually) and then instructed him to leave the dressing on for as long as possible and when that time arrived, to return for further attention and if need be another dressing. Then he bought several bundles of firewood off him and gave him half a crown, showing deep concern especially with the feeling (in those days) that such a deep wound between finger and thumb could (it was believed) easily cause Lockjaw. Also, there was Spot the culprit to consider, a family member, well loved, especially for his fearless spirit. We didn't want to lose him so it was extra special that the police or authorities should not know. The young man returned a few days later and showed a well and truly healed hand, thanks to the wonderful ointment.

Spot however did have his favourites which fortunately we all were. Another was someone called Cecil who at some time or other had seen Spot stung by a wasp and was limping badly. He called Spot and holding his paw extracted the sting then treated the sting with Reckietts Blue so that as he walked, he showed a little blue foot. Spot never forgot, on one occasion Cecil called Spot from almost half a mile away and Spot responded with a huge burst of breakneck speed finishing up by jumping into his arms. I held my breath, but it was unnecessary. Spot loved him.

Another time my brother George was opening a bottle of beetroot wine an old lady herbalist had given him and as he released the cork it made a loud hissing sound and the contents started whizzing up the neck of the bottle. In a second Spot leapt and seized George's trousers at the waist band ripping them totally to the turnups. George was hopping about shouting "No Spot No" but it was too late. He dropped the bottle in the sink and lost the lot. No one could point a finger, hiss or simulate a weapon of any kind with Spot about. A burglar, gunman or murderer wouldn't have stood a chance. This same dog would sit with me on a winter's evening and allow me to dress him up in collar, tie and hat.

My Mother with Spot

My most embarrassing moment, though it wasn't at the time (I knew no better) was when on a Sunday evening we were together alone in the house and Spot was laying on his back, legs up in the air and I noticed something and was terrified. I thought Spot was dying and I ran all the way to the Llandudno Spiritualist church where my father and mother were attending. I ran full pelt up the stairs and crashed through the doors into the service, dashing to my mother crying out "Spot is dying." My mother guided me outside and listened to my sort of explanation. She soothed me immediately by saying "No he's not dying love." I understood from her he was O.K. and sure enough he was. Apparently although I didn't know 'til years later he was fantasising, and it seems I was a startled witness to his fantasy.

He died eventually after being poisoned by someone who we think we knew and as he lay on the kitchen floor, the cat passed very close to him and even in those dying seconds he wrinkled his nose to challenge.

Summer

After coming to live in Llandudno in 1930 we seemed to have the most wonderful summers. I never owned a heavy coat only a Sou'wester with a Sou'wester hat for the rainy weather and in that year I was by the pier looking at a family dancing round their beach hut with a hand wound gramophone playing *"Amy Wonderful Amy,"* a song composed and became something of a hit because of Amy Johnson's solo world record breaking flight, from Britain to Australia in nineteen days. Another song of the day the record of which could be bought in Woolworths for sixpence was *"Wheezy Anna."* It was 92 degrees in the shade and the people drunk, not with alcohol but with Amy Johnson's achievement.

Within a short space of time I was enrolled in the Infant's School at Morley Road, Craig-y-Don, the head mistress being a no nonsense silver haired lady who if she needed you for some correction or other wouldn't think twice about hauling you out by your ear, but despite this she was a good woman, a good teacher with high principles and determined in every sense of the word. My recollection of the infants is cutting out patterns with blunt scissors and sometimes trimming each other's hair with remarkable results and writing with a slate pencil on to a slate that was encased in a wooden frame.

I was at some time or other persuaded to join the National Savings and somewhere I still have the original pale-yellow savings card with two blue sixpenny stamps on it. The stamps must have been bought under duress or pressure for it was never added to. I wish now, remembering how valuable sixpence was then, that my mother who I suspect was responsible for buying them had used them herself, for today it's not worth the card it's stuck on.

I quickly collected friends around me. George who lived with his widowed mother and sister Lizzie who married a jobbing builder who only had a motorbike and sidecar to handle everything he needed and yet despite this he eventually became one of North

Wales' premier builders and brothers John and Tom, their next door neighbours Sheila, Edna and Alec, all about my age whose father was a builder.

Other pals were Alan a useful cricketer who I always tried to select on my side. He always hit sixes in place of their singles. I knew what I was choosing. Stanley was another. His father played the drums, his mother the piano and his mother's sister the violin and together they were capable of singing and entertaining an audience. I used to climb and sit on the wall and peer into the entertainment arena which was in effect a very long wooden hut at the back of the Bedford Hotel in Craig-y-Don.

Girls in my life, (not actually) but those of my own age who I remember. Ella, who as an exception in those days had dancing lessons, deportment and voice production. I remember her in the old church hall next to Dunphy's in Craig-y-Don performing the routine of Ginger Rogers and Fred Astaire, tap dancing and singing to her hearts' content dressed in a fairy like white fluffy outfit. Joan and her close friend Dorothy and Beryl whose father kept a little shop where I know you could buy a pennyworth of broken biscuits, because I did so once but in a larger quantity after looting my money box of sixpence in pennies with the aid of a dinner knife to extract the coins and when my mother found out she really told me off. I think now, it may have been considered by her as a secret emergency fund though that was very far from my thoughts at the time my thoughts were nearer my stomach and the luxury of having biscuits some of which must be sweet, creamy or chocolaty. Even now my mouth trembles at the thought. There are others too whose names elude me, but they still frame a picture in my mind. Oh yes! There was John another friend whose house we moved into later when he moved away. There was also a best friend at the time, Tony. We had no end of scrapes and scraps together but immediately following any fall out we were knocking on each other's door wondering if they were coming out.

One time I found a metal spring stiffener out of a woman's corset and bending it, I offered it to Tony as he sat on his haunches on the top of the brick wall at the entrance to my father's workshop in Curzon Road. Releasing the stiffener, it sprang out hitting Tony on the nose, causing him to fall off the wall. But next moment he was at my house asking if I was coming out.

Another time in Victoria Street I was on one side of the narrowish street and he was on the other side with a half house brick in his hand threatening to chuck it at me. I was dancing from one foot to the other challenging him, so he threw it. I dodged and the brick went straight through the bay window of the house I was standing in front of.

The brick landed on the table where the lady was doing some ironing. She sort of fainted from shock and meanwhile my friend was hurtling down the street, shouting "Don't tell her where I live." I seem to remember my dad being responsible for all repairs and apologies.

Unfortunately, Tony and his family moved away. I only saw him once again some years later when we were both about thirteen and almost strangers to one another. I met him by accident outside the Post Office in Craig-y-Don.

At the side of Pearson's grocery shop in Victoria Street, there was an entry which turned at right angles and ran behind the houses in Victoria Street. At the other end it turned again at a right angle back into Victoria Street. At this end was a gable end of a house against which was a telegraph pole at the top end of that were ceramic insulation cups and I was throwing stones up at them. The stones were bouncing off the gable end, back over the width of the entry into the back garden of the house opposite and in the process was damaging and breaking the glass in a greenhouse. For this escapade I received quite an admonishment from my father.

I'd be about eight or nine years old, already a voracious reader. I'd read the story of the Greek guy Icarus with the waxen wings who wanted to fly like a bird, but the sun melted the wax and he fell to the earth. Fired by this story, I found a large umbrella in a rubbish container behind the Grand Theatre and I repaired the damaged struts by tying and binding them with my father's upholstery twine, and then struggling somehow, I climbed onto St. Paul's church and jumped off. Unfortunately, as soon as I jumped, the umbrella turned inside out and I dropped like a stone, damaging the slates of the vestry roof but fortunately missing the joists as my legs went through the roof. I was apprehended by the Choirmaster, an elderly chap with white hair, who was constantly on the look-out for new choir boys and had already tackled me two or three times in his quest, but this time he was on a winner, so he thought and I was forced to attend choir practice the following Thursday. I can see him now walking up and down with a tuning fork in his hand, occasionally stopping until he came to me when he stopped again. This happened two or three times then he suddenly said, "Right you can go home." That shows you how good my voice was. You know, I've looked at St. Paul's since, quite recently and I haven't a clue where I jumped from. I have a feeling I climbed a ladder and then jumped from some sort of flat surface. I am wondering now if they had some kind of scaffolding up.

My father (*pictured left during the First World War*) initially worked at Leaches corner, situated diagonally opposite St. Paul's in Craig-y-Don, but later started on his own, his workshop being in a garage at the back of our flat. Later still he moved to a workshop in Curzon Road, Craig-y-Don. The premises consisted of two very large rooms which ran over and above the garage. At one end there was a flat that was occupied and one of the windows of the flat looked over and onto the roof of the garage as did the toilet window in the workshop.

The two workshop rooms were very large and ran at right angles to each other, approached by a staircase from the front door at ground level. The first room was used mostly for storage, the second room, the workshop. To the right on entering this room there was a toilet block. In the centre of the work room but to the right-hand side there was an old-fashioned stove with the chimney running vertically up through the glass canopy of the roof. Around the stove there was a metal cage with a 6-inch metal wall around it to catch the ash and cinders to avoid any fire risk. In winter this stove was so hot that the actual chimney pipe at the stove end used to glow red hot (these were real winters) and it was possible to melt the old-fashioned metal curtain rail simply by thrusting it into the stove.

My brother George (*pictured right*) and I used to hang empty one-gallon tins at the far end of this room with a mattress hanging behind to absorb the impact of our pieces of lead strip that we made into "shot" for our catapults. This was done usually after work or at weekends when dad wasn't present.

On my own, on one occasion I borrowed an air gun from someone I knew and I was firing out of the toilet window, over the roof top of the garage below, at some socks that were hanging on a little washing line belonging to the people in the flat. The next day my father met me as I was entering the workshop, mounting the stairs, on my return from school, which was just around the corner. He said he'd been accosted by the tenants of the flat who complained of picking lead pellets out of their wall-papered room. I was suitably reprimanded but on reflection believe I was aware of a slight glint in my father's eyes.

I guess the worst time was when I got my hands on an old bus tyre and was determined to use it in place of a hoop, which was normally an old bicycle wheel with the spokes removed and with which I used to run miles all over Llandudno and I believe that may be responsible for being as fit as I am today. I suppose I may have had the feeling of one-upmanship by trying to use this huge tyre which was taller than I was. Anyway, I managed to stand it upright, and then in front of the admiring eyes of one or two mates, I started it rolling, firstly with a wobble, then with the aid of the hill, it began to move faster and faster. Suddenly, I realised I could no longer keep up, though I was running at top speed, the gap ever increasing and to my horror realising it would reach the main promenade road that ran along the sea front. By now the hill was easing but the tyre wasn't and for some reason it lurched to the right for which I was initially pleased about because it meant it wouldn't go onto the main road but to my despair I watched it mount the pavement and in airborne flight saw it disappear through the ever open door of a seasonal little round wooden building, which sold everything a holiday maker may have required, lemonade, ice cream, apples, crisps, tomatoes even. When I reached the door and tentatively inquired if I could have my tyre back, I was met with what I thought must have been an earthquake. The shop was a mess. The counter was overturned. Everything that had been displayed on it was now all over the place and staggering to his feet in the midst of all this was the shopkeeper. Four letter words were not the norm in those days, but he used all the others, so I decided to forget the tyre especially when I could hear him shouting after me. "I'll get yer - I know your father - You wait."

The result was I received a good telling off with a graphic description of what might have been if luck hadn't had been on my side. My father had to make the shopkeeper a new counter. I don't know whether it cost him anything in money terms, but I've no doubt it cost him a few drinks in the pub. Paying that way seemed more agreeable than paying hard cash though it very often in my father's case was more expensive.

A great time as a child was bonfire night arriving annually but starting weeks before by me and the other lads, collecting rubbish (on my father's hand cart) and forming on the beach a huge mass of rubbish, trees, boxes, furniture, anything at all that could be set on fire. No messing with Health and Safety in those days. It was a time which I looked forward to immensely and whenever I could afford to, I'd buy a halfpenny banger or Jacky- Jumper from the newsagent in Craig-y-Don, ready for the big night.

About this time, I was persuaded by a couple of pals to create a Guy, a stuffed figure of a supposed Guy Fawkes. We also obtained from somewhere an old type bath chair that consisted of a wicker constructed armchair-like seat with a steering handle that controlled a single front wheel with large spoked wheels at the back and side of the chair. The Guy was placed in the chair and part of the system was to call at houses and ask for a penny for the Guy. We were pushing this contraption around St. Margaret's Drive in Craig-y-Don and knocked on a door. The lady that answered with just the hall light for illumination was confronted by this grotesque corpse-like figure. We, being smaller and hardly visible behind the rear of the seat and the figure of the Guy were suddenly aware of a half-stifled scream. We hurried away as fast as we could. The following night I heard my father reiterating this story, with a chuckle. Apparently, she hadn't been very well lately, and our Guy Fawkes didn't help. I think it may have caused a relapse.

Those were the wonderful times when days were never long enough. If it wasn't games like top and whip with a halfpenny flyer on the flat square of a surface behind the Washington Hotel, it could be hide and seek in the dark with only the street gas lamps to help you, or marbles, or footer, or cricket, or conkers and sometime or other a bow and arrow, self-made of course and a catapult or a hoop, never ending running with a spoke less wheel off a bike, or a four wheeler despite my later gashed ankle, or perhaps a kite. (I made one of these but lost it in the sea). Or roller skating though this came a little later when I was slightly older, when we used to play hockey on skates on the smooth flagged area of the paddling pool in Craig-y-Don. We also used to skate as fast as we could by the shelters and jump off landing some fifteen or twenty feet away on the pebbly beach. Unfortunately, this didn't do the wheels much good, what with the impact on landing and the sand that that got into the ball-bearing wheels. Fortunately, I was able to buy spare wheels off an old chap who used to come around with vegetables on his horse and cart two or three times a week and on alternate days would sell fresh fish direct from the sea on the back of his cart. When I say fresh, the fish were still moving about. He was also a bit of an entrepreneur and would buy anything that he thought he might be able to sell; hence my roller skate wheels which he bought from a bankrupt skating rink, and which I got for three pence each. Another time my mother bought tiny wooden boxes of figs off him which she used to stew or chop up in rice pudding to help sweeten it instead of sugar. He said they were ship-wrecked stock from some vessel that had sank but the little boxes were so well made and lined with some sort of silver foil that the sea water had never affected them. This was wartime, remember. This old chap would deal in anything that he could lay his hands on.

One of my favourite childhood haunts was Castle-Rocks and to get there it was necessary to walk up Nant-Y- Gammar Road, turn left at the top, passed the quarry on your right, up what was the Gravelly Hill until on the right hand side of the road there was a metal gate. Enter and walk along the steadily rising path, through the trees, looking down to your left onto Bodafon Hall and Tea Rooms. Continue until emerging out of the trees, shrubbery and shadowy image into daylight and green grassy slopes and there before your very eyes is the hard rock face of Castle-Rocks, climbable with foot and hand holds, with grassy plateaus on its ledges - wonderful! Almost eighty years later in 2015 I visited Castle Rocks again and my heart sank. It no longer was the same. In place of the grassy area there was now shrubbery, trees and all sorts of wild vegetation growing, totally destroying the vision and memory.

Further on and the environment though still hilly becomes flatter and you pass many types of trees, but before that there is one glorious view that will last in my memory for ever, the two bays in the distance, Llandudno Bay, West Shore Bay and the Conwy Estuary with the castle in the background, a picture that is worthy of any artist's creation. But now back to the trees, amongst them, walnut trees. Any connection to eating was always a big temptation and on this occasion I was hurling a wooden stick into the trees trying to dislodge the walnuts and whilst doing so was suddenly conscious of something or someone and I turned and saw the clothed figure of one of the gamekeepers running towards me. Whenever that happened, I never asked questions. My only answer was to run, which I did and after some seconds or minutes running over the uneven grassland, which is tiring, I looked back thinking I'd outpaced the gamekeeper. To my horror there was a hand reaching out for me, not two feet behind. From somewhere I became the possessor of rocket power. I accelerated and kept on, frightened to death, leaving the grassland behind me dashing eventually to the main road that leads to Deganwy on the left and Craig-y-Don and Queens Road on the right, still not looking back or slowing down. At last I came to my father's workshop, the key in my hand, opening the door still not looking round until I arrived upstairs, the door slamming behind me, then at last, looking through the window and thankfully seeing no one outside. I'd outpaced him. Incidentally this was in the summertime and we were now living in Victoria Avenue, Bryn Tawel (House of Peace) and to allow my mother maximum vacancies for visitors, my father, brother and myself used to sleep in the workshop and explains why I had a workshop key.

I had another altercation with a Mr. Humphries. He was a notable architect and designed amongst many buildings the Post Office in Vaughan Street which is now a protected building. He lived in a magnificent bungalow overlooking the sea. My brother George was working there prior to the war attending to the black-out of the bungalow. Other workmen were there doing jobs whilst he was away on his holidays, leaving the manservant or butler in charge. One of the workmen was actually chopping wood up in the lounge close to a silk carpet when the manservant intervened and said "Mr Humphries won't be very pleased. That carpet was handmade specially, by a family in China and cost over seven hundred pounds." Considered to be a fortune in those days.

But to return to my altercation. You remember the entrance through the metal gate after passing the quarry with the hill like mountain on your right, well we as lads used to climb to the top of this mountain then roll rocks down watching them gathering speed until hitting the flatter area in front of the wire fence they would bounce up into the air, clearing both the fence this side, the road between and the fence the other side, finishing up careering into the field behind. On this occasion who should come along in his Rolls Royce but Mr. Humphries. This time he emerged from his car after a boulder had whizzed over the road in front of him and made to give chase but obviously hadn't a chance and eventually returned to his vehicle brandishing his fists. So ended another escapade. In 2015 when I visited this area, I was again disappointed for the hillside which we had previously rolled boulders down and sledged down was no longer there. It was covered with vegetation, shrubs the lot. Completely spoiled.

One of my most cherished childhood memories was, I think it was in 1937 was sledging down the slopes through the metal gates near the quarry, on my home-made enamelled Colman's Mustard advertising sign. I stopped at the very bottom of the slope and directly in front of me on the grass was one of the new six or eight-sided three penny bits which had just been issued in time for the

Coronation. They'd only just been announced and here it was I'd found one. In modern talk "I thought I'd won the lottery."

Another equivalent find was on a Saturday. I believe it was at the time of the Duke of Kent's marriage to Princess Marina, I think it would be 1934; I'd be nine years old. The whole country was celebrating and on the waste ground at the back of our home I found a blackened disc which I took home and with the aid of some Brasso - elbow grease discovered underneath it was a bright lovely sixpence. Phew! This was a magical moment, a whole sixpence. I know I walked on air along the promenade towards the pier bouncing almost with every step.

Christmas

Christmases weren't they lovely? Three of us, carol singing like foghorns. At one house, at the top of Queens Road towards Deganwy. We'd sung our opening lines when one of us said "There's no one in." I with sharp eyes said "There is. I saw the curtains move." I quietly pressed the flap of the letter box open and bent down to look in. The moment my eyes reached the level of the opening and peered in, I found myself looking into another pair of eyes only an inch or two apart from mine. I dropped the flap hurriedly and whizzed off down the path but at another house we were rewarded with the huge amount of one shilling which was more than we'd collected all night. (I think he paid us to go away). At 9 o'clock or thereabouts we were returning passing the same house when one of us suggested we call again, this time singing a different carol and to make it more convincing we swapped scarves and one moved his cap onto someone else's head. Lo and behold, the same gentleman came to the door and once more gave us a shilling. I think our takings came to ten pence each that night. The greatest financial success we'd ever had. On the way home I called at the Premiere sweetshop, which was still open and bought my mother a bar of Bourneville plain chocolate, for Christmas, the next day. She liked plain chocolate and I still think that was the greatest gift I'd ever given anyone, and it still pleases me to this day.

My father especially at Christmas always visited the British Legion Club and nearly always won something at the raffle. Before I was born, I believe he won a live Flemish Giant rabbit which became a family pet and used to sit up for a drink of coffee. My mother tells the tale, one day, Bun, which was the name of the rabbit (short for Bunny), escaped into the street. My mother chased after him and was just in time to see, a large dog further down the road, racing after him. Bun, stopped, turned and raced back to my mother, standing in the middle of the road shouting "Bun, Bun, Bun" and Bun succeeded in reaching her to safety, by springing into her arms. Funny things animals, so often underestimated, misunderstood then suddenly by this sort of happening, being understood in a way that might well have been absent before.

One year my father won an enormous box of Cadbury's chocolates measuring about one yard by about two foot. There must have been eight or ten pounds of chocolates in it, all lined up in rows. When mother finally opened it (she tended to forget for a while) but my prompting reminded her and once it was opened and on the go, it meant I could secretly take one or two chocolates out, without, I thought, being noticed, but my mother mentioned more than once there was a little mouse, a two legged one, in the house who'd been getting at the chocolates.

My brother Sam and Mary, (later to become Sam's wife) and her parents used to stop with us at Christmas and on Christmas morning we always had some gammon with the breakfast, the only time in the year we had it, but it was from Pearson's little grocery shop and Mr Pearson had above his shop name the words "Ham and Bacon Specialist" and he was. It was possibly the best that money could buy.

Somehow or other my dad would always try to obtain a bottle of whisky, and it was added to the morning cup of tea, occasionally at night-time too. My mother (I can see her now) when the bottle was empty used to swill it with a spoonful of tea, so as to not to waste the whisky. It's a habit I still do myself this very day and each time I still think of her with wistfulness and tenderness.

Sam contributed throughout the year to a Christmas club and at Christmas would bring us a large box of Cadbury's Chocolate Drops and a large round tin of Jacobs's shortbread which was in layers of triangular shaped portions which again enabled me to have one or two, disguising the loss by shuffling the shortbread about and do you know one day when I was at the paddling pool a chap came up to me and said "You've got a brother in Greasby, haven't you?" I said "yes" in surprise. "Sam's his name, right?" I nodded totally amazed. He said he recognised me by my looks. When I told Sam about this sometime later and described the man, he said it was the son of the lady, who ran the Christmas club, but even he was surprised, and I don't think I looked anything like my brother.

When I was about seven or eight years of age I made myself a four wheeler out of a plank of wood and some old pram wheels and I was trying it out on a noted hill, Romania Crescent in Craig-y-Don, speeding down it when the front wheels lurched into some fault in the road surface, this threw my feet off the axles either side of the plank which was the steering system. My left foot encountered the whirling front wheel and in doing so acted as a brake. When I stopped, I noticed a huge split in my Grandma's (Dad's side) hand knitted woollen socks and as I was examining them, horror of horrors, I was suddenly conscious of a large pool of red liquid. Blood that was mine. I could see a gaping blood-filled gash just above my left ankle bone. No noticeable pain. Everything must have been deadened by the deepness of the gash. At this moment the brother of Cecil (Spot the biter's friend) appeared on an errand bike. He worked for Parry's the grocers in

Victoria Street. He grabbed hold of me and sat me in his empty front basket. With my feet hanging over, he returned me to my father whose opening remark was "Good God. What have you done now?" But with his supreme confidence, after a swift examination and the comment "stitches are needed and quickly," he got me to the doctor's whose surgery was a few doors away from "Kestin" the flat we lived in. From there I was transported to his other surgery at the opposite end of the town just across from the pier.

Apparently, the doctor's equipment was there. I remember him remarking "a fraction lower and you'd lose your foot" then the brass wire as he threaded it through the flesh pulling the wound together. Then about ten days later having the wire removed by snipping and pulling the strands out of the flesh as it knitted together. I have two visible scars and this one figured on all military identification documents.

Birthdays

When I was ten, on my birthday I was the recipient of a brand-new Hercules bicycle. A present promised by my eldest brother Sam several years earlier when I must have been moaning about wanting a bike. He said he would get me one when I was ten. Before that, I was too young he reckoned, and he was undoubtedly right although I thought differently at the time. On the morning of my birthday there was no bike and I went to school totally disheartened thinking I'd been forgotten. At dinnertime I called at my father's workshop and he and George my other brother were busy working. "Has it come dad?" I asked in a melancholy voice. "Nothing at home son?" Then after a moment or two he said, "Have a look in the toilet." I entered the toilet where the wash basin was and against the wall was a shape of two wheels and a frame; the handlebars were twisted in line with the frame (for easy transportation) and all of it was wrapped in brown paper. In those days the whole of the frame, handlebars etc were wrapped in a strip of two-inch-wide brown paper which was twisted round and round the parts of the bike. For a second I looked and then the jubilation, the knowledge that Sammy hadn't let me down. Always his word was his bond. A promise, even an expression of intent was never forgotten, always kept throughout his life. The following Sunday my brother George (older than me) said we'd go for a ride and we started towards Conwy travelling one side of the river past Trefriw, on to Betws-y-Coed and then we went wrong, intending to travel back to Llandudno on the other side of the river but instead travelling some twenty miles or so more that we wanted to, passing Capel Curig, Lake Ogwen and on towards Bangor and along the coast road through Penmaenmawr and Conwy back home, travelling the last hour in total darkness without lights and apart from this I was sore and didn't participate in long rides for a good while after.

It was about this time and age when I featured in a play performed at the Arcadia Theatre on the promenade. It was produced by our schoolteacher, the daughter of a man who had a butchery business in Penmaenmawr. She also played the piano in the production and I was one of the Imps (admirably cast.) There was about twelve of us as far as I can remember and Cecil with his head of wavy ginger hair was our master and on his command spoken three times "Sacha Wacha Wiska," we trouped out from the wings on each side of the stage and performed some sort of dance which meant lifting our feet well up into the air. My shoes, the only pair I'd got had just been repaired, not with leather. My father had used Congoleum, like roofing felt but with a painted pattern on it, mine being a light blue background with a daisy pattern on it, fully visible to the audience, as I learnt from my mother afterwards.

A short time later I was riding along the Bodafon Road with a pal on the crossbar. When we approached the incline that swept down past the quarry, I let everything go and peddled like mad. Tragically the road surface in front of the quarry was all granite gravel and the moment we hit it at full speed, the bike keeled over and my pal hit the gravel with me on top and we travelled in this way for fifty or sixty feet before coming to a stop. My pal's leg was severely gashed, and the hip side of his body was in a bad way. I was severely bruised and grazed my left knee and took all the skin off my left arm, but I was more concerned about my bike. The front wheel was like a letter S and immediately thought of Sam and his warnings of being careful.

A couple who were picnicking in the quarry rushed over and commenced bathing my pal's injuries with pure whisky. For my part my father bathed my grazed surfaces with Boracic Powder in the water, then after drying, anointed the wound with the wonderful healing ointment, Vaseline, Zinc and Boracic ointment mixed in equal parts, the ointment being laid on fairly thick then left for a few days or until the bandage or dressing worked loose and when that happened the dressing would contain all the muck from the injury including the bits of gravel and the injury itself would contain a new pink skin - marvellous. I don't think it is used these days.

I've seen nothing to compare before or since and now after some two hundred years or more of boracic ointment being used, some researchers have come up with the notion that Boracic ointment, or powder or crystals should never be used. When you consider the benefit, it served for those poor souls who suffered from the effects of mustard gas during the First World War. Before this ointment was devised, imagine the pain and suffering experienced especially by a Scottish kilted soldier who could be burned from the neck down to the very base of the spine by mustard gas, resulting in a huge puss laden blister covering the whole area of his back, which had to be cut open to allow the puss to escape...then the healing, the scabbing which on commencement of healing would crack and reopen with every movement of the body. Then the life saver was discovered...the cream, Zinc, Vaseline and Boracic. The Zinc to dry the wound, the Vaseline to soothe and heal and the Boracic to sterilise and cleanse the wound. The ointment would be put on with a spatula, a large one and spread thickly over the burnt and wounded area, and then a clean dressing would be applied and left untouched, contrary to today, until it loosened. When the dressing was removed how wonderful to see no scabbing just a wonderful new pink skin and all the muck and mess removed with the dressing.

I have used this ointment throughout my life and can vouch for its wonderful healing qualities. A few years ago, I saw the latest petroleum based dressing which was provided in a sealed package and which I was told cost five pounds each time it was used and was changed at least once every day but which couldn't compare with the ointments I have written about. I understand today they are using a type of spray which sets like a skin over the burn and prevents the air from getting to it. I don't know any more than this but until I know more, I will always doubt its capabilities against the Zinc, Boracic and Vaseline.

Entertainment

Raymond had a brother Jacky and several other younger siblings. I knew Raymond and Jacky well; they often featured in our cricket games and so on. Their father was a jack of all trades and worked at The Grand Theatre, which was then a picture house, a cinema. He did everything including posting the billboards throughout the town. He also had a wonderful insight into television an almost unknown factor in those days. He built a television set which worked. His job was not particularly well paid, and the family suffered many setbacks including his own illness which kept him from working for several months. Another time, the whole family was struck down with Scarlet fever and each room in the house was covered with drapes to fumigate the property.

When the Second World War started, the BBC took over the Grand Theatre and many programmes were broadcast from there. The resident organist who gave frequent daily broadcasts was a Scot who used to dash from the Washington Pub on his auto cycle, run into the theatre and jump into action on the organ, always breathless from enjoying his whisky and leaving it until the last minute. It was in the Grand Theatre well before the second world war that I saw the first entertainment I ever knew and I can remember queuing up in the cold winter evenings, huddling in the queue under the glass veranda for shelter from the icy wind or the teaming rain to see Laurel and Hardy or Joe E. Brown at their peak, sometimes Felix the Cat a forerunner to the cartoons that would soon be invented by Walt Disney and would sweep the world in the form of Minnie and Mickey Mouse, Donald Duck and all the gang.

The Grand Theatre is situated in a quiet spot halfway between St. Pauls Church in Craig-y-Don and the North Western Hotel which is the start of the town end of Llandudno. Around it, there was just a bus garage at the side nearest the town end, which lay back also very quiet and was hardly noticed. For the rest of the way up to the North Western Hotel, it was more, or less waste ground only occupied with a large billboard advertising the forthcoming films due to be shown in the Palladium Cinema. The only other building in that area was a roller-skating rink which became the latest craze following the Yo-Yo and the Biff-Bat which had come across from America, the rink was situated almost next to the North Western Hotel.

Oh, the Yo-Yo and the Biff-Bat do you remember them? If you do, you're from the same era as me. If you don't, think what you've missed. Woolworths used to have a wooden dais placed at the end of their long wooden counters and on it would stand a young lady dressed in a pure white sweater with the words Yo-Yo or Biff-Bat emblazoned in red across the front of her sweater. She would perform all the tricks of either one or the other, her short white skirt swinging from side to side as she danced to the movements of her white plimsoled feet. I think Woolworths gave it up eventually as it began to effect sales. Most of the customers were more interested in watching the demonstrators.

On the opposite side to the Grand Theatre was a huge area of allotments (my father had one) and alongside, a large area of grassland on which football or cricket could be played. At the side again was the Llandudno Town football ground. This area today is a vast retail park featuring all the usual retail stores and outlets.

I met Tommy Handley on one occasion on a particularly stormy day. He was standing in the doorway of the Grand Theatre with his dog, a lovely large Labrador. He was doing his best to pull his fawn coloured trench coat around himself, trying to shield the wind and rain that was lashing down. He commented on the weather in such an ordinary casual way. At the time I couldn't as a kid, grasp or understand how someone so famous could be so ordinary. He was a nice chap as I remember him.

Kestin

After a number of years living at "Kestin" a friend of my mother's, had to move to Northwich because of her husband's work and we decided to move into her house, not very far from "Kestin." My mother also took on looking after a lady who was badly affected by Rheumatoid Arthritis and had no living relatives other than an elderly retired female cousin living in Wolverhampton. My mother then took in visitors as most houses did in Llandudno.

I shudder and marvel today when I think of the work she used to do. She had no help other than the bit that we did for her. On one occasion she had twenty-two visitors, with the two top bedrooms doubling or tripling up, to help several young girls from the Potteries, so that they could have a good holiday. Nothing was of trouble to her. She fed them 'till they almost burst, entertained them and always had a smiling face. She used to say these people have saved up all year to come on holiday and the last thing they want to see is a miserable face. I had to help with the washing up, reluctantly, I must admit. I wanted to go out to play with my mates, cricket, football, skating and so on and when one set of dishes was completed and I thought I was ready for off, lo and behold another course of dishes would appear, to my moans. Remember in those days every morning each visitor had to have hot water taken up to their room and always with a cup of tea and at the weekend, Saturday when holidays finished and began, immediately after breakfast as soon as the visitors were out of the way, bedclothes were turned back, newspaper liberally sprayed with genuine American turpentine, then inserted in the beds with the sheets covering them, then left for as long as possible before changing the sheets. At such time the bed would be scrutinised by my mother and if any fleas were present they'd be drunk as my mother used to say, overcome by the turpentine and no longer able to jump, then each, if any, would be crushed between finger and thumbnail, then the beds would be remade with fresh clean sheets ready for the next intake.

Towards the end of the season my mother would be asked if she could take in any theatrical people who might be appearing in the Pier Pavilion or the Arcadia. One of these was a lady who was playing a Scottish maid in a play with Winifred Shotter, the play being "The Divorce of Lady X." This lady always had prunes for breakfast and after a few days she asked my mother if she required more prunes. When my mother said, "No there's enough for the week," she replied with astonishment "I've never known them last so long."

Another theatrical person who stayed with us was Norman Griffin an actor manager who starred in "Tea for Two" at the Arcadia theatre. (That was the name of the song that featured; I think the play was called "No No Nanette" and I'm sure Anna Neagle starred in the film of the same name). With Norman Griffin was a young woman, the relationship was in doubt, but she had wonderful large hazel coloured eyes and she knew it. The first time my mother spoke to her she looked over my mother's shoulder staring so that my mother could see those eyes in all their glory. My mother who could be quite mischievous and droll at times, turned at first to look at the wallpaper behind her, thinking perhaps a seam had come loose.

One thing that was obviously apparent was the constant work that the actor's manager had to do; for each night after the show he would be typing letters, for future theatre bookings, accommodation for the cast and reading plays for future productions. He never seemed to rest.

Regretfully, the Arcadia Theatre is no longer there. It was demolished and in its place was built the warehouse like building now known as Venue Cymru. I remember someone saying they had seen seeing Paderewski, the world-famous pianist performing in the Arcadia. She said the piano was arranged for him on the stage, a stool positioned for him and when he appeared from the wings, clad in evening dress, walking slowly to the piano and then sitting and rearranging the stool for what seemed an eternity during which there wasn't a sound, you could have heard a pin drop and then he started playing the most magical music, the whole audience breathless, enthralled until the finish when the applause was like thunder.

My own recollections of the Arcadia are of two speciality dancers who lodged for the summer season in a flat above ours at "Kestin" and had colossal rows, throwing crockery at each other and so on, yet on stage they would each emerge from opposite wings, move rhythmically round and meet with a kiss in centre stage.

The other memory I have is during the war when the Arcadia was full of servicemen. This was when nudes were first allowed on stage, providing they did not move. In this show they appeared in various postures, each set in a large picture frame, so that one time they were facing one way and the next they were facing the other. Now the seating in the Arcadia was a central arrangement being the conventional stalls; to the right and left of the stalls the seats ran outwards to the outer walls of the theatre sloping downwards from those walls until they met the gangway either side of the centre stalls, consequently it only took a minute or two for the servicemen to realise which way the nude was going to face, this led to a general exodus of the stalls to the appropriate side which gave them the best view. I've tried to make this as palatable as possible but there's no disguising the ardour of youth.

Relatives

I believe my father was one of nine children and I only know of three, Aunty Bessie, Uncle Gerald and Aunty Mabel. Aunty Bessie was a large figure of a woman, full of joy and giggles despite having a hard life. She would sometimes pop in on us at Llandudno unexpectantly, which was the accepted form in those days. She always greeted my mother in a half gallop down the hall, her arms outstretched and finishing in a bear type hug and the words "Oh! Beaty. Oh! Beaty," not much more but so full of feeling. She died in Chester Hospital with what I think may have been stomach cancer. She left a husband, Uncle Bill, a daughter Eunice, two sons, Ernest and the youngest Norman who I finished up being called after.

Uncle Bill used to visit us at odd times in his seventies or eighties and would sit in the corner of our kitchen, by the black leaded grate, a pipe in his mouth, not saying much but observing with studious eyes and one day after studying (in my opinion) for some time, he said to my mother as she passed by in full throws of working as usual. "By God Beat that lad has got some legs on him. They'll serve him in good stead." I'd be about ten or eleven at the time, but those words reverberated with me on more than one occasion in my life as you will see.

Eunice, his daughter never married, she was in service a common practice in those days. Later when that sort of employment was disappearing, she became a housekeeper to a retired Lieutenant Colonel and his wife who lived in Chester and later due to the wife's alcoholism moved to Bull Bay in Amlwch, Anglesey, almost in isolation. Living in a building that had previously been a chapel which was now joined to a building next door purchased and dramatically increased the size and obviously must have suited the Colonel for the life which they were now forced to lead. Later when it was generally assumed he would outlive the wife, he died and, in his Will, left Eunice a sum of money provided she looked after his wife until she died and when that eventually happened Eunice was again granted a sum of £500 for her services. When the relatives of the Colonel and the wife all got together in Anglesey after his death, Eunice approached them suggesting that if they would agree to it, would they allow her to keep the property and forfeit the £500, which they were all delighted to do, apparently it saved them a lot of trouble selling the property and sorting things out. Eunice then turned it into a guest house and Freda and I and the children had some wonderful holidays there. All the meals were more than ample, and she had repeated visits from so many. She was an excellent cook and fish, crabs, lobster were all fresh, straight out of the Irish Sea the same day as being cooked. On occasions when we were there, seated at a large table in the company of a Solicitor, Works Engineer, a Doctor and a Chief Executive and the conversation was ongoing, lively, interesting and all with their families. I loved it. The conversation was sparkling.

In the hallway, Eunice had a life-sized stuffed Alligator, about six feet tall. It stood balancing on its tail and hindquarters. In its chest was a little door, which when opened revealed all the cleaning kit required for polishing your shoes. Visitors would frequently pose with the alligator for photographs. This and loads of other thing in the house were given to her with the property.

One item was a diary compiled by Lieutenant Colonel who was the first man into Tibet, under a penalty of death if discovered and led the party that our Lieutenant Colonel belonged to. The diary "spoke" of so many hardships, catastrophes and tragedies. Crossing torrential rivers, losing men and horses. Fever and disease prevalent. All written about in a matter of fact way which suggests they were almost used to these happenings.

Eunice was a careful woman, emptying the ashes each night at the top of the garden and reclaiming them next morning to back up the fire. She couldn't tolerate waste, but this same woman was generous to the extreme.

Her father, Uncle Bill was an old grouse, for despite Eunice buying him a house which was a replica of the smallest house in Great Britain which is in Conwy and which cost her one hundred pounds early in the nineteen thirties, after Aunty Bessie had died. On being shown around the house which contained everything that was needed for one person, Eunice said "There you are Dad and you can decorate it to suit yourself." (He was a painter and decorator in his working life). He replied, "If you think I'm going to do this up you're mistaken."

Later, Eunice had a room built on to her kitchen, which was a self-contained unit so that she could keep her eye on him. Her dad lived until he was ninety-four.

A point of interest; my father had an Uncle Bill who it was said, one day in a sudden unexpected move got on a train at Chester and decided to go wherever the train took him and it finished up in Jarrow where he eventually became Mayor of Jarrow.

The youngest in my Dad's family was Uncle Gerald who as an adult became headmaster of the largest school in England situated in Erith in Kent with over a thousand pupils. When the second war broke out he was selected and responsible for the organizing and evacuation of all the children in the London area for which he was awarded the O.B.E. Incidentally I being the youngest in my family was supposed to be named after him, but on the morning of the christening Aunty Bessie turned up and persuaded my mother to christen me Norman after her youngest and so here I am, Norman.

Early Life

When I was about ten years of age I was taken with my father and my brother George on a short trip to the Isle of Man for George to see the T.T. Races. Had George have lived, (he died aged 26) I know for sure he would have done his utmost somehow or other to have competed in the Manx Grand Prix in September when most of the riders were independent amateurs, private enthusiasts who raced for the love and thrill of it with no financial backing whatsoever. We had to travel to Liverpool to catch the Mona Isle, the ferry that sailed to Douglas at 11 p.m. Arriving at 6 o' clock in the morning, we went into a cafe on the front that had a huge hot plate with dozens of fried eggs and bacon and fried bread for 1/3p loaded on it, all ready for the masses coming off the boat. After breakfast and a short rest on the prom we started walking out of the town to take up our positions before the roads were closed for the actual race. Our objective was Craignybar and Hillberry. My memory also takes in my brother George at 19, extremely self-conscious and shy, helping out several young ladies by piggy backing them across a muddy corner of a field into a position of dryness and comfort, leaving me to fend for myself. (It was one of those things I could rib him about later as and when the occasion arose.) The great riders I remember was Stanley Woods on his Velocette, Jimmy Guthrie on his Norton, the great motor cycle of the era and Jock West riding his BMW; always recognisable by the twin cylinders sticking out either side, and Walter Rusk riding a Velocette, I think and Crasher White a schoolmaster who rode in the amateur T.T. in September. Jimmy Guthrie was killed whilst racing in Germany and I believe there were crowds at his funeral in that country. The sport and the sportsmen overruled all political differences at that time.

After the race we made our way back to Douglas where we had to wait until late in the evening for the return ferry to Liverpool, so to pass the time away we went into a cinema on the promenade. The film was *"Dead Men Tell No Tales,"* and featured Emlyn Williams (a great favourite of mine) and Marius Goring. After the film I mentioned to my father that it was funny having no news or short films. Apparently, it had, but I'd fell asleep during it. We'd had very little sleep during the previous forty-eight hours.

George and Sam

And now my two brothers Sam and George. There were three actually, but the first one died as a little baby.

My brother Sam and George were both older than me. Sam as a baby was earnest, quite solemn almost adult but somewhat stubborn and difficult at first to handle until mother with her wisdom found out the way to tackle him, because if Sam said "no" he meant just that and wouldn't budge. Mother's method was to create and relate a story with a moral in it, a parable if you like. She would say years later. She would see the tears well up in his eyes as she would come to the ending and then he would straight away go and do whatever previously he wouldn't do.

As a brother, Sam's word was his bond. If he promised or said he would do a thing it was always honoured. His life was entwined with honesty, helpfulness, guidance and trust and with a huge knowledge gained from reading and experience, so much so, many people were perplexed, amazed and couldn't believe it when they saw, heard and watched him, often from afar. He was an icon of majesty with his work, apprenticed as a plasterer, but studied hard on the side, winning a silver medal for all Great Britain for his work in artistic decorative plastering and mosaic work taught to him by the masters in Italy.

George my other brother, was the quiet one, very sensitive, quite slow at school, but on leaving thrived and grasped knowledge that had previously been unknown to him. Again, a good son, a good brother, one who I had arguments with, laughs with and always was a wonderful accomplice. He never had much money and probably realised the value of it more than most because of the lack of it. Despite this, I remember, he saved up, after my Dad had gone to Stourbridge and bought our mother a warm winter coat. It was greyish white speckled tweed. I remember it well and my mother thought the world of it. She never had many things given her and this, I know became a treasure and she wore it for many years and even afterwards was kept with love and safely in the wardrobe.

George had a great passion that was motor-cycle racing. He saved to go to the Isle of Man T.T. races, meeting Sam and Mary (Sam's wife) there on one occasion. He used to give his all on a Raleigh racing bicycle, racing flat out in a demonstration and fantasy of the real T.T. thing.

I became the object of much of George's experimentation and jokes especially whilst we lived at "Kestin." Two of which are as follows; -

The owner of "Kestin" had a parrot which was fastened by a long harness to a stand and George introduced me to the bird by shaking hands, the finger being offered to the bird which went through the motions. In my case though, it promptly took my fingers to its beak and removed a neat 'V' shaped piece of flesh from one of them.

George also introduced me to electricity (long before Health and Safety was thought of.) He offered me a large mattress needle which he suggested could be magnetised by touching one of the brass fittings in a broken light switch. This I did and promptly dropped the needle and yelped with the shock. George had watched the electrician doing this many times and he was so used to it the shock it didn't bother him, and he could stand it with no sign of discomfort.

George was a keen woodcarver and had been given as a gift a set of old English chisels by the widow of a chap who was a woodcarver by trade. These chisels were made of unpolished steel, all priorities being given to the edge and keenness of the cut and for the lasting qualities of the sharpness. The handles were of finest cherry wood. George for some crazy reason had placed a half inch chisel in his inside jacket pocket, had entered the Post Office, dropped something, bent down to pick it up and the chisel penetrated his chest between his ribs. He was immediately aware of the warm rush of blood that surged out of his chest and clutching his trousers around the waist, trousers which that had been father's and was extra-large at the waist, which acted in this instance as a receptacle, like a bowl, in which to catch the blood. He made his way back to the workshop where now white in the face he emptied his waist trousers now full of blood into the ashes surrounding the stove. My father's reaction was "What have you done?" Then followed a quick examination, which to the satisfaction of both showed no lung or organ penetration but my father was alarmed at the huge loss of blood. He quickly obtained from somewhere or other some colostrum. It's the first milk that the cow gives after the birth of the calf and its value in nutriment is priceless. Added to this was liver as a food intake accompanied by rest in bed. Within two days he was back at work with only a half inch healing scar to show as a reminder.

Two other little stories which happened whilst we were living at "Kestin" which as I've mentioned before were let out as flats.

In the top flat there lived a retired Vicar and his wife and they had a cat which for some reason or other basked in the wonderful summer's heat, on the stone windowsill. So comfortable was the cat and lost in the warmth of Summer that she or he turned over and rolled off the windowsill, dropping four or five storeys to the ground. This happened three times, each time landing on its feet, just shaking itself then walking off unscathed.

Another wonder story about cats was when we lived at in Victoria Avenue we had a she cat called "Kit" who had kittens regularly almost in the gestation period of eight weeks and the custom then was to keep one kitten of the litter for the mother and if no homes could be found for the others they were usually drowned. It was a different world then, a harder world in many ways. This was the general practice which my mother didn't always follow, the result being "Kit" finished up with quite a few kittens. My mother finally said she couldn't manage with them anymore so George who was reupholstering a three-piece suite for a farmer in Penmaenmawr suggested that he took "Kit" and her offspring to this farm where there was plenty of mice and birds, so they wouldn't starve. He took them as he pushed the suite on a handcart and dropped them at the side of the road by the farm. When he returned my mother asked him about the cats (she was really upset about the decision) George said "Kit, the mother just sat in the middle of the road and looked about her. The others dashed into the hedges and ditches." Ten days passed by and there was a terrific commotion at the back of our house and our dog "Trixie" a replacement for old "Spot" the biter, was barking like mad. Mother went to the back door, opened it and saw this thin, dusty, travel worn cat, dash under the dog's belly and then moved in and out of my mother's legs purring like an organ. It was "Kit." She'd travelled all the way back about ten or twelve miles which included crossing the river Conway. Mother kept her after that. She couldn't get rid of her again. "Kit" drank a bottle of milk and slept for two days.

Such was the substance of my brother, George who was called up into the Welsh Guards, weighing just nine stones and returning on leave after three months weighing twelve stones and having gained one inch in height. That's what a difference the Army did for him with fresh air and exercise.

George died on the 4th of June 1942 aged twenty-six, with two others whilst climbing the cliffs at Ilfracombe in Devon. He was buried in St. James's Church, Wollaston, near Stourbridge right at the forefront of the church. His tombstone stands there today in very good condition and I try to see it at least once per year, usually on Armistice Sunday, together with my Mother and Fathers who are buried together, in an unmarked grave at the rear of the same church.

Fishing

When we moved from "Kestin" to Victoria Avenue I'd be about ten years of age and I believe I'd left the hoops and the tops behind and was more into football, cricket and roller skating and a little fishing mostly on the beach at Craig-y-Don, usually in the evenings, sometimes fishing in the dark in the belief that the fish bite better then.

I made my rod from a penny bamboo cane obtained from Bevan's the ironmongers. The reel I got from a mate, I swapped something with him. I bought the metal eyelet loops through which the line ran, from Westmorland's, a small shop on the opposite side to the Town Hall. I fastened them and the reel by binding them with upholsterer's twine. The lead weight was made by melting lead into an empty old Colman's oval two penny mustard tin and inserted into it, was a metal loop to which the line was fastened. Armed with this I'd go on the beach and I quickly learnt to cast out a good distance which ensured the likelihood of catching more fish, as the water was deeper. Usually it was whiting, not too large but delicious to eat, so fresh and sweet, also dabs and occasionally small eels which I always threw back never fancying them.

Sometimes a local, Dr would come down also to fish and he would nearly always ask in his broad Scottish accent "How are you doing lads?" He was a fine doctor caring deeply for his patients, though was often terse and to the point. I remember one time, another pal of mine had something in his throat and his father who was a cobbler, working on his own, wouldn't leave his business to take him to the doctors so I said I'd go with him. We stood in the surgery as Dr examined my friends throat. "Open your mouth," he said as he held his head with one hand, then tilting his head so that he could see more clearly but my friend moved his head apprehensively each time the doctor tilted it. "Keep your bloody head still," Dr suddenly barked. My friend became instantly rigid as the doctor removed the offending fish bone from his throat. The same doctor visited our home each week to see that the lady my mother looked after, was well.

On one occasion he came, and my mother had a severely lacerated arm from some sort of poisoning in the skin. She was discomforted to say the least, but she'd got visitors to look after and although the arm was bandaged, she also wore a long-sleeved dress or blouse to help disguise the problem. However, after visiting the lady, Dr would always announce his farewell and at this time noticed the bandage and insisted on having a look. When he saw the state of her arm he said "Good God woman. How long have you had this? You should have come to see me. You must keep the arm out of water," and he prescribed a cream which did the trick and he never even rendered a bill. In our time we heard of many similar facts about this man.

Although I fished mostly off the beach because it was free, I once paid, to go on the pier, thinking deep water, more fish. There were several grown up men as well as me. One of them had a brand-new Greenheart rod which at that time was the finest on the market. He'd rested it sloping on a bulwark at the edge of the pier overlooking the sea. He'd fixed a bell on the top end of the rod so that it would ring the moment he had a bite. Meanwhile he was sitting with his back against a bench eating a sandwich. Another, with his penny cane stood at the edge, swinging his rod back and forth in order to get a good cast out to sea as far from the pier as possible which was always the ambition. As I cast, so my rod hit the sloping Greenheart rod and it rocked and swayed dangerously towards the sea, balancing just about on the bulwark it was leaning against. The owner grabbed the rod, then me, cursing and clouting me behind the ear.

We continued fishing in more or less subdued silence until I was reeling in to check the bait on the hook, when suddenly I'd got a bite and I hauled in a magnificent Pollock, a deep water fish that must have spotted my line and bait as I was reeling in and chased it, resulting in me being the only one that day to catch anything, with a penny rod and next to a Greenheart. It provided four good sized steaks and a huge scowl from the Greenheart owner.

My greatest memory of fishing is with my father and mother and brother George, I'd be about ten years old, it was in March and my father decided to hire a rowing boat and we set off into Llandudno bay, eventually being way out into the Irish Sea and looking back, the hotels were the size of matchboxes. It was about 4 o'clock in the afternoon and within twenty minutes or so the sea changed from a normal swell to waves of such height and depth. One minute we were sixteen feet or so up in the air, flying almost, the next we were down in a huge trough of turbulent water with nothing above us except sky and walls of water. The boat was being tossed around like a piece of driftwood. My father was already in his shirt sleeves' battling with the sea and the oars, the boat was leaking, and he ordered us to look into a small cupboard at the rear of the boat for tins or anything to bail the water out. Sure enough we found some and started bailing for all our worth. We finally arrived back in the calmer waters of the bay at nine thirty at night and just as we approached the jetty where the owner of the boat was waiting one of the oars broke. I thought my father would go mad at the owner when he asked for payment for the oar and I remember his words vividly. "You're damn lucky you haven't got four lives to account for with your leaking boat and your rotten oars." Such is the power of the Irish Sea when it turns nasty.

I have never ventured in a rowing boat since due undoubtedly to that experience though I do like the seaside. I also witnessed on a couple of occasions, bodies being recovered from the sea and have never forgot the pale bluish cast of the lifeless bodies as they were brought to the shore. One of whom was a man about twenty seven years of age who suffered from sleepy sickness and who under doctor's orders had to bathe in the sea daily as part of his treatment, often when he was talking to you his voice would suddenly ramble off gradually into silence and he would rock gently on his feet, to all onlookers apparently asleep. I was never a swimmer. My only other experience of saltwater was crossing the paddling pool at Craig-y-Don on stilts for a bet. The bet was only verbal, no money entailed and unfortunately halfway across, the stilts slipped on the slimy surface beneath the water and I fell off fully clothed losing the bet.

In 1926 my father was returning from the Isle of Man and there was a huge storm, one of the worst in living memory so I'm told. It took sixteen hours for the ferry to return to Liverpool which is normally a six-hour journey. My father, who was a good sailor, never sick, but he said he held on to a stanchion for the whole of the voyage. There were women in fur coats lying in vomit sprawling on the deck, clutching on to anything they could, just wishing to die. No crew were available they were all absent, below deck, due to their own sickness, and when they finally docked in Liverpool some of the women were heard to say to those who were waiting to embark on the return journey. "I wouldn't go on that boat for all the tea in China and those women looked visible wrecks." My father immediately aimed at having a drop of whisky at Jimmy Annas, a pub, (I think that's what it was called,) to settle his nerves, so he said, but he was unlucky, the General Strike had just been declared and everything was shut down. For ten days afterwards the bed just went up and down like the motions of the ship. This story of the conditions of the crossing was confirmed to me years later when I heard it mentioned on the television as the worst Irish Sea crossing ever known.

At the rear of our house in Victoria Avenue there was a piece of waste ground on which we used to play, light fires, roast potatoes etc. Eventually part of this ground was sold, and a large hotel was built on it. When it was being built and was about one storey high, one or two of us were climbing over it after the workmen had gone home and I jumped from one wall to another which had only been built that day and as soon as I landed on it, part of it fell to pieces. I was horrified and quickly looked to remedy the damage. I found a piece of slate and a quantity of mortar that hadn't gone off and I replaced all of the broken section back to its original state. As far as I know my repair was never detected and the hotel is still there to this day and is called The Dorchester.

During construction, myself and Basil another pal who lived just a few doors away used to chalk wickets on the wall and each of us would take turns at batting whilst the other bowled. At one time when I managed to escape from the washing up, I dashed out knowing that Breezy would be waiting for me. Sure enough he was and as I ran, he shouted something and hurled what I thought was a red leather cricket ball, so I dashed forward to catch it. It burst in my hands. It was a large tomato and covered me. Breezy couldn't bat for a while. He couldn't stand up he was helpless, laughing so much.

At the rear of the Dorchester there were steps up to a square plateau, an area outside the hotel's kitchen. It was used by the Chef to cool things off or to allow them to set. One time I had to retrieve Trixie, quietly, unobtrusively from the plateau, after she'd devoured a number of trifles, all in glass dishes, put out there to set, standing on trays ready for the evening meal. There was no refrigeration in those days.

Another time I literally had to pull her out of a large meat tin. She was standing in it, four paws deep in dripping. We always suspected Trixie of having worms or something rather than a good appetite, though we never had any proof of this.

Shillings and Sixpence

When I was about eleven and had moved to Llandudno Central School in Trinity Avenue, I was approached by the daughter of a seventy odd year-old widower who ran a grocery business in a small shop in Victoria Street, to become their errand boy. To deliver by bicycle the groceries that people ordered and required them to be delivered. They paid me ten shillings a week, an enormously generous amount, as the maximum others were paying was about seven shillings and sixpence. This was typical of the family, they not only lived good lives but in every way they were the essence of what Christians should be. They were a wonderful family which also included another daughter, unmarried, who worked at Baxter's the photographers in Vaughan Street.

Florence was a woman probably in her forties who worked in the shop and virtually ran it for her father, who also worked full time in the shop. The story went that Florence was engaged to a young man who lost his life in the slaughter of the First World War She never married, and someone lost out on a wonderful person.

The shop owner had a hearing impairment and to compensate for this he had a huge circular bell connected to the telephone and more than once I've seen customers in the shop virtually collapse when the phone rang. It was like the sound of "Big Ben" but with a quicker beat.

I used to work from half past four when I finished school 'til about 6.30 to 7 p.m. I used a bike with two big baskets, one over the front wheel and the other over the back and I travelled all over Llandudno at different days of the week, from the Little Orme to the West Shore. One of the deliveries I used to do every week was to Sir William Letts's house. Lady Letts was actually old Mr. Pearson's sister and she has the same genes, kind, warm, friendly, considerate. No airs or graces and did no end of good, charity wise.

She helped the Scouts, the Cubs, and the Girl Guides. A lovely person and do you know they only had two children, both boys. One was killed in the First World War and the other was born with a disability, but because they were well off financially, they were able to keep him at home with them, under the guidance of nurses employed full time

This is one of my loveliest memories almost Dickensian. Each week I would leave my bike halfway up the drive whilst I walked the rest, to the rear of the house. Knocking on the door a middle-aged motherly type Yorkshire woman would answer and would accept the delivery from me. She was spotlessly clean in a white starched apron, her hair neat under some spotless white headgear. "Would you like a drink of lemonade?" she would ask. "Yes please," I would answer breathlessly. (I didn't really have lemonade. Often, I would have a bottle of water with sugar in it and shake it up.) To taste the real thing was heaven and I went to heaven most weeks. She would then say almost as though it was an afterthought, but it happened every week. "Would you like a piece of cake?" It would be either sponge or fruit. I could only nod my head; my mouth wouldn't function only when the huge luscious slice was held in my hand then entering my mouth. I'd walk back to my bike in a dream, fantasizing what it must be like to be rich and to have cake like this every day. At Christmas that was even more special. I knocked on the same door and the same lady would answer but this time she would say "Please come in, follow me, Lady Letts wants to see you." I followed, solemn, serious, quiet, in wonderment. Out of the kitchen, down a red quarry tiled passage, carpeted with a royal scarlet runner. At the end was a large hall or foyer in the middle of which there was a table and behind the table Lady Letts was standing, bowing towards me as if I was someone of importance. "Hello! What is your name?" I'd tell her, and then she would ask in the most delicate tones. "What school are you attending? Do you like it? What does your father do?" Then a series of other questions not inquisitive, indelicate or intrusive, but with interest and concern. Finally, she would thank me for all the times I'd delivered to her and taking a packet off the table on which there seemed to be dozens. She'd wished me a Merry Christmas and to my family, placing a package in my hand then replacing that with a gentle handshake as she spoke the words of greeting.

This package contained five shillings, two half crowns, the largest sum of money I'd ever received up to that time in my life. I didn't walk down the drive to my bike. I skipped, floating on air, delirious with riches beyond my wildest dreams.

I continued in this wonderful employment until I left school at the age of fifteen and a half to join a firm of Accountants as an Articled clerk.

School

But before that let me tell you about school, Llandudno Central School, I remember one teacher we called Cowboy because of the way he caned; whirling the cane around his head rather like a lasso before it descended in a whoosh to frighten the life out of you. One day he was a bit late attending the class and of course there was a lot of talking and noise going on when suddenly someone said "he's coming" and a hush fell on the class and we could hear the steps racing towards us, then the door opening and his entry, with eyes bulging. He had the whole class out and caned the lot, but he was using psychology in his application though we didn't know it. At first he would miss your finger-tips by a fraction the, cane fairly screaming by, your own action being to draw your hand back out of the way, but when it finally hit you it didn't seem on reflection to be quite as bad as what it had sounded like a moment or two before. However, he was a good teacher who was very patient and would go over and over a problem until you understood it and acknowledged that you did so, but if you didn't understand and said you did, this would really make him mad. His results with pupils speak for themselves. They all did well under his guidance, but probably the one with the greatest influence which I've recognized more vividly each year that my life has gone by was John Gwilliam Jones a strong Welsh Nationalist who taught English but who wouldn't write in anything other than Welsh. This man who every year won the principal prize at the National Eisteddfod for Playwriting and Drama was described by Hannen Swaffer a leading critic, in the thirties, as the *"Ibsen"* of Wales and who pleaded with him to write in English, but he never did. He even translated many of the classic English and Irish plays into Welsh for performing.

Mr Gwilliam Jones was the man who gave me a new perspective, a love of literature, drama and theatre and it all started when the class had written an essay on several options. Billy a classmate and friend of mine faithful and honest with a sardonic sense of humour, one time showed, in an essay, a simile he said the character was so chuffed he looked like a pleased schoolteacher, Mr Gwilliam Jones's eyes glinted at this, returned to his desk and resumed marking, then called me out. I rose hesitatingly, standing as far away from his desk as I thought it was possible to get away with and far away enough to avoid the flying book which I thought might be coming my way. Instead he summoned me to his side. Then seeing the headmaster passing the classroom door rushed and ushered him into the classroom, all the time speaking excitedly in Welsh, pointing at my exercise book, finally the head patted my head and in Welsh I gathered he said, "Well done, very good." I'd chosen for my essay *"The Hobo Remembers"* and I'd written "the hobo remembered the shivery winter," and the word 'shivery' was circled in red and in red the word excellent written against it. My new world had begun. I had a new understanding, a new insight, a new perspective into the beauty and power of the English language, and this intensified when I discovered the theatre. I believe owned by a Lancastrian playwright whose Repertory company performed week after week in the Pier Pavilion. I believe they had three companies, one in Rhyl, one in Llandudno and the other, in Aylesbury. One of the casts there being Ronnie Barker, learning his trade.

I have never seen any theatrical performance match this repertory company in any degree whatsoever and it was undoubtedly down to good actors which Armitage Owen chose for that reason, but more especially to a wonderful creative producer by the name of Noel Morris. This man could turn a pebble of a play into a diamond. His ability in this direction was amazing and gave each of his productions the edge over any other producers who were likely to direct the same play. I have never seen plays since that can compare in any way with Noel Morris's productions. Not only did he extract everything from an actor, but he also changed their movements, even to the way they walked. In fact, he aimed at the character in the play being absolutely realistic He insisted and aimed at this, so as to convince the audience of the authenticity of the character and he did this week after week. Tragically Noel Morris died in his early forties when he was already being spoken of as a future head of the National Theatre. The theatre, I am convinced, lost someone who would have enhanced any production he was concerned with, in terms of light years. Billy Donohue and I used to go every Saturday night to see this Repertory Company, and often the plays we'd seen were discussed avidly the whole of the following week by those who had seen it, such was the power of them.

One of my greatest memories of this company was watching a performance of *"Suspect,"* a play written by Reginald Denham and Edward Percy, the lead being played by an actress named Wynn Clark. I must say here. I have never seen anyone faint on stage or film like Wynn Clark. She crumpled to the floor as though held by invisible strings and when she hit the floor it was imperceptible, no sound, no noise, just a sobbing figure of a broken woman. As well as being a good actress it pointed to that man again, Noel Morris.

It was announced in the local paper the following week-end that Wynn Clark, that very day, (when in the evening we'd seen the play) she had received a telegram from the War office announcing the torpedoing of the battleship The Prince of Wales and the loss of her husband. It was the 9th of December 1941. What a player. What an actress. What a woman.

Another fine actor of that company was Noel Johnson who had recently been discharged from the Army after receiving injuries during the evacuation of Dunkirk. The injuries left him with a bad limp which somehow or other he managed to disguise when on stage. He played every conceivable part from old men to young men, very young as for example Danny in Emlyn William's "*Night Must Fall*." Some years later he starred on radio as Dick Barton Special Agent as well as many other roles in Television and Cinema.

Another great memory of the Manchester Rep. A play called "*Daddy Longlegs*," adapted from a best-selling book written by Jean Webster. I have never seen anything so electrifying as this, so tense, so breath-taking, so suspenseful, so memorable, in a lifetime of theatre going and who was responsible for this, as well as the actors, Noel Morris the producer I've seen no one to compare with, ever.

Employment

Reluctantly I must move on from the Manchester Rep and Llandudno Central School and that little grocery shop and enter instead when I was fifteen and a half the professional offices of John, Henry Hibbert, Certified Accountant, Chartered Secretary and Structural Engineer, an orphan brought up by Dr Barnardo's Homes, becoming Chairman of Llandudno District Council before the advent of Mayor's.

He was a great humanitarian. At one time I was called upon to announce the arrival of an old lady who was behind with her rent. At the same time Sir Mathewson Watson, a great friend and ex workmate of Sir Harry Lauder the theatre and Vaudeville artist arrived, and I announced this to Mr. Hibbert. He said, "Show Mrs So and So in and tell Sir Mathewson to wait." I duly showed the elderly lady in and in a gentle voice he escorted the lady to a chair, his hand gently resting on her shoulders until she sat at ease. Then he listened to her tale of woe and then said "Now don't you worry. Your rent is fifteen shillings per week. From now on try to pay that figure each week. That will stop your arrears from growing. Occasionally when you have a little bit to spare, pay sixpence off and the arrears will start to come down. Is that alright?" She stood up her troubled expression replaced by a smile of happiness. "Oh, thank you I'll try to do that every week" and she left the office all despondency lifted. The next moment he'd say in an entirely different voice and with a flourish." And now we'll see Sir Mathewson." He entered and was met by a personage as different as chalk and cheese, to the one who had dealt with the old lady. His humanism was terrific; he could speak to a Lord with authority one minute and with a down and out with humility and understanding, the next. His letter dictation was a treat. Pipe smoking, walking gently up and down the carpeted office floor speaking clearly, without hesitation, only for punctuation for the benefit of the secretary, and the result, letters of class, distinction, brevity if need be, or longer if necessary but created by a master. Incredible.

David was a partner in the practice. When I attended the interview, he was introduced to me and I thought he'd stepped right out of a Dickens's novel. He wore dark jacket and dark grey pin striped trousers. His expression I thought was dark and brooding. Never was I more wrong. He was a quiet guy, fond of cricket and his wife and their little child. Always conscious of everything going on and very fair. Now and then I had to go with him for an audit to Caernarvon and one time I missed the train, so I searched Llandudno for an alternative quick means of getting to Caernarvon thinking I would likely get the sack. In Back Madoc Street, there was a large garage with huge floor space and I reasoned there might be Reps or travellers as they were called in those days, which would be forced to stop the night and in so doing might leave their cars in this garage for safety reasons. Sure enough there was a middle-aged chap who said he could give me a lift to Bangor where I could catch a bus to Caernarvon, so I accepted the lift and arrived at Waterloo House in the square at Caernarvon about ten minutes after him. He looked at me with a grimace and said, "You lucky beggar, if that had been me, they would have been going anywhere except Caernarvon." He added with a twisted grin, "I was just about to get your cards ready." I think he was secretly pleased that I'd shown initiative or whatever.

On the station returning to Llandudno he went to the toilet which he'd also visited in the cafe at dinnertime where I'd partially disgraced myself by nearly choking with laughter when one of a group of Welsh speaking farmers, whilst shaking pepper, the top came off the pot and a great mound of pepper landed in his soup. Returning from the toilet, which incidentally I hadn't been to all day, he said "What's up with you, you must be a bloody camel." I immediately saw the connection, but probably blushed and shrugged my shoulders. I was quite shy and reserved in those days despite my determination, but I'm sure you can see the humour in the man.

This is the man who supplied me with a copy of The Argosy monthly publication of the world's best short stories, all of which gave me a further insight into the power and brilliance of the written word and later, the spoken word.

The rest of the staff at J. H. Hibbert's was Tydwen who was mainly David's assistant and worked in his office although she was also in charge of the main office where I was, with Kathleen a typist, Mr. Griffiths an Audit Clerk and later another chap from the Manchester area, whose name I can't remember but who was an exceptional good and well experienced accountancy Audit Clerk. Together we used to visit the Penmaenmawr Electric Laundry, which was situated halfway up the Penmaenmawr mountain, the office where we worked in, being a glass, greenhouse type of building situated in the centre of the laundry and was exceptionally hot. The owner was an elderly man who was always present and in attendance, extremely smart, clean and pristine, who wore gold rimmed glasses, this man was certainly a gentleman in every aspect.

Another chap who joined the office, ended up becoming a good pal of mine. We used to have a lot of fun together. A great moment for me was when we used to collect rents together on a Monday and we used to call at his house wherein he had a stock of pre-war fruit drinks and we used to sample them. They were gorgeous, there's nothing like them today.

I was about sixteen at the time and one of my jobs was to light the office coal fire in the morning and any other little jobs that might come up. On one occasion I was asked if I could clean the keys of the long carriage on the Royal typewriter because the print was appearing a little fuzzy and wasn't up to scratch for balance sheet work. I was given this puttylike substance which was used to press on the keys to absorb some of the fluff and dirt and someone remarked, "there was a little black brush somewhere for brushing the keys" and that it was probably in Kathleen's desk. I promptly in all innocence asked Kathleen who was about seventeen, "If she'd got a little black brush in her drawers." There was a deathly silence, for what to me seemed an eternity, sufficient to allow the blush to cover my face and for a colleague, a man in his forties, to emphasize my question to the girl by saying. "Well go on, you heard what he said have a look." My memory is of pure discomfort. I don't think I spoke much the rest of that day but kept my head down desperately avoiding eye contact especially with the female members of the staff.

I think it was a different age then. It certainly was for me.

On rent collections on my own, I used to travel on foot, from one end of Llandudno to the other, West Shore and to the last two houses on the Great Orme. To get there I used to walk up the tram track backwards from Church Walks where the tram started from. I thought it was easier walking up the hill in this way rather than the conventional way. When I was close to these two houses, tenanted by two ladies both with three or four kiddies, no end of times I would see the a little lad dressed only in his vest and he would shout upstairs to his mother, "Mam, the rent man's coming "and she would say, "Tell him I'm out." When I arrived at the door the little lad would say "Me mother says she's out." I would then respond by saying "Right. Well tell her to bring it down to the office," and fair enough she did.

On my downward descent in Church Walks I would call in on my good pal Billy Donohue. He went to my school, in the same class and we were firm friends. I used to walk up the side entrance after descending the Great Orme and together we would have our own feast, eating bunches of grapes whilst sitting on a stone whitewashed wall in the smaller greenhouse surrounded by vines, hence grapes. We were living it up. Billy Donohue was in a reserved occupation for a while but then had to join up. He was killed in France when a mortar landed in the trench he was in. I still feel the loss to this very day.

I remember Billy and I can't help smiling as I do so. Determined to ride his bike along the jetty towards the open sea and nearing the end, thought he could turn round on the bike on the three or four foot wide jetty, but when he did so the bike slid from under him on the slimy surface and he and the bike finished up in four feet of water. Walking back dejectedly, wheeling the bike, a lady at the promenade end of the jetty said, "Oh! Dear, are you wet sonny?" Words failed him.

I have a huge guilt factor relating to Billy which haunts me to this very day. When I was in Normandy, whilst activity was still feverish, I received a letter from Billy's mother after she'd lost her son asking me how I was and telling me that Billy's younger brother was now nearing the age when he would be called up and she was fearful of what might happen. I could sense she was looking for reassurance, help of some kind to see her through the trauma she was facing, I don't know whether this feeling is retrospective but to me it is, because I never replied to that letter. I was nineteen years of age, young and maybe foolish. I had certainly not realised fully at that time the love between a mother and her child even though that child in this case was approaching manhood. I was thoughtless and inconsiderate, and I deeply regret the lack of action on my part, for the memory of it reappears time and time again in my mind. I have other guilt factors here and there, of a similar nature which in retrospect I put down to youth, inexperience of life and the feeling that you have, at that time, of everlasting life. You feel you'll go on for ever. These factors, not too many, recur time after time in my memory especially as age overtakes me and the biggest and often the most horrific "thing" is time on your hands when you can think too much.

I also used to call, collecting rents, on an elderly lady who lived in Bryn-y-Bier Road, West Shore. She was ninety-four years of age, was always in bed in the bottom bay windowed room in the house. Her son left the rent money on a dresser by the side of her bed. As soon as I knocked a voice which strengthened every second bid me to come in. She was waiting for me every week and as soon as I entered the room "Sit down" she'd say, waving to the chair. She'd waited all week for me, for company.   Loneliness is the biggest enemy of widows, widowers and elderly people. "And how is little Johnnie?" she'd say.   Little Johnnie was my boss, J.H. Hibbert, himself, about sixty years of age, she remembered him and everyone else coming to Llandudno with very little possessions and she filled me in on every one of them. This lady knew most things and nearly everyone especially those who had made a fortune since their arrival. She was lonely. She wanted someone to talk to.   A problem that we have today and will become more predominant as the population gets steadily older.

Chapter 2

The War Years

When I was seventeen- and three-quarter years of age I received a brown inconspicuous envelope, inside of which a card stated that I must report for a medical examination in Caernarvon in preparation for call-up. That would be round about January 1943. In March on my eighteenth birthday I received my call-up papers to report to Brecon in South Wales on the 1st April. This I did despite the fleeting temptation to say "April Fool" and not go. The same day my hair was savaged and the same afternoon we were taken on a run by the Physical Trainer, a hardened regular army sergeant. The main memory of this apart from the panting run was the tune of the day *"You are my Sunshine,"* which we were encouraged to sing whilst returning to camp marching at ease and in the shower afterwards. I had never been in a shower in my life and when I turned the thing on, it first of all nearly scalded me, then when I rapidly switched it the other way it almost froze me. What with gasping and jumping up and down I reckon I did more exercise in the shower than I did on the run.

After six weeks training, mainly drill we were tested to see what we were suited for, the idea being no "square pegs in round holes." The idea originated in America and was the brainchild of psychologists and boffins and featured a patterned floor similar to a hopscotch set up. It was necessary to move as quickly as you could around the patterned floor in a set order against a stopwatch.

My test was good and was the fastest on the day which was evidenced by the looks on the faces of those others taking the test. The sergeant tester looked at his watch disbelievingly and muttered "it can't be." He shook the watch and said "you'll have to do it again" which I did, but obviously shattered by the first attempt my second was much slower but still passed the level they were looking for; accordingly I was sent to the 59th Training Regiment at Barnard Castle in County Durham and inducted into the Royal

Armoured Corps for six or nine weeks training (I forget which.) Afterwards I would be posted to either a Tank Regiment or an Armoured Car Reconnaissance Unit.

My first parade and memory was of a certain hard-line regular Army Sergeant Major who on inspections would wave his baton within an inch of your face. When he faced me, he barked "What's that on your face? Are you growing a moustache?" I knew I had only one answer otherwise I'd be on a charge for not shaving. (Up to that time I hadn't) but I was aware there was the beginnings of a moustache on my upper lip, so I had to answer "yes." "Well shave it off" he bellowed, "then let it grow, then shave it off again and again until it looks like a bloody moustache, not like a bloody hedgerow blowing in the wind." That's when I started shaving.

One of the lads in the same intake was a tall blonde who thought of nothing but cricket and managed to miss loads of duties because of his ability in that sport. After the war he played for Somerset. His son later also played for Somerset and represented England in Test matches. His grandson is doing very much the same today, representing his country even now as I write.

Another chap, was an actor and understudied Richard Attenborough in his first big part as *"Pinky"* in the crime thriller *"Brighton Rock."* He would on occasions think nothing of uttering the famous lines from Henry the fifth, which with his rich voice boomed and echoed throughout the barrack hut.

As I was talking to him, don't forget I was only eighteen, very impressionable and an ardent theatre goer, especially with the wonderful Manchester Repertory company productions which I'd been privileged to see at Llandudno, he told me of several incidents in his theatrical life, some serious, some funny. I can't remember too many but I do recall him saying that on his first walk-on part with words to say, he had to enter the stage from the wings - stride across the stage and say "Madam, the safe is open and the cash box is stolen." Unfortunately, when he crossed the stage he tripped over a mat and said, "Madam the cash box is open and the safe is stolen."

When performing P.T (Physical Training) which happened daily we would be paired off with anyone who might be opposite you at the time and given boxing gloves. We would then have to "have a go" at each other for several minutes. I was never very good at this. I sort of didn't like hitting the other guy. Anyway, I was chosen to compete in an inter squadron boxing tournament being held in another camp, a couple of miles down the road. On the appointed night I was I was teamed against a guy, who was a former circus clown, and later after our fight became a contender for the British Army Championships. I seem to remember as an amateur the rounds were of two minutes duration and three rounds in total. Well as I said I wasn't much good unless I had a cause or reason to fight for and at this time I had no such cause or reason and I was severely hammered coming out of the event with two huge black eyes and into the bargain.

The next day I was on guard and was on parade on the main square, with a cold wind blowing; my two eyes streaming with the swelling and the wind, when a murmur ran from one to the other "He's coming." He being the R.S.M. (Regimental Sergeant Major) Six-foot-tall, straight as a die, body like whipcord, dressed immaculately, trouser creases like a knife edge, face pallid without expression, eyes steely pale blue. You could sense every soldier growing by half an inch in anticipation of being inspected by the most feared inspectorate in the regiment. He stood bolt upright before every man, his eyes like gimlets, searching, examining, ex-raying, looking for details, and never speaking, never known to, until he came to me. He stood before me. My gaze straight ahead, avoiding eye to eye contact but looking through watering eyes, tears running down my cheeks in the bitter cold air. "Are you alright, soldier?" The voice was quiet and unpredictable. Never had it been known for him to speak on parade before, unless it had been for levelling a charge on an individual for poor dress or such like. I replied, "Yes Sir." He said as he moved off, "Good turnout," which apparently, so I was told had never been said before. I learnt afterwards he was on the front row of the boxing hall and had witnessed my annihilation, and my continuation to the end, which must have some way, impressed him.

After about five weeks of training I broke my fibula and tibia in my left leg just above the ankle on the Assault Course. The instructor told me to make my way to report sick. It was the last period in the afternoon. Sick parade was at 6.30 p.m. If you missed it then that was it, so I walked as best as I could taking my small pack with me, toothbrush, paste etc which always had to be done. I missed my tea and can almost feel the hunger even now after all those years. I managed to get there in time, just.   That night I was moved to a large military hospital at Catterick Camp, Yorkshire. Now for a little while I won't be writing much about the Army, but at the same time it must be spoken of, for the people in the scenario are so real, so talented, so wonderful, so unforgettable, I couldn't at any price forsake them. They were truly remarkable. Now for the setting - Hollywood at its best, even better because I was a witness to it. Unforgettable.

It was a long ward, possibly twenty beds each side with a wide spacious centre between them, everything spick and span, gleaming with cleanliness. It was in the days of the Matron. There was a central door at each end of the ward which led into other areas. Toilets, washrooms etc at the one end and at the other a large hallway from which doors led to other wards, rooms etc. At the hall end, about five beds away from the doorway slept George but this morning he wasn't sleeping. I was in a bed on the opposite side at the far end away from him and I was just lifting my plastered leg out of the bed when I heard the voice, this wonderful Italian tenor type voice singing *"Funiculi-Funicula."* I wanted to look at him, but I was concerned he might be shy and might stop so I hesitated until he hit the high notes and when he sailed over them I turned and looked. George was sitting up in bed, arms outstretched in song and the end of the ward was thronged with nurses, sisters and doctors who burst into cheering and clapping at the end. It was like a scene in a film.

A day or so later I was transferred to Hauxwell Hall, a country mansion and estate in Yorkshire that had been taken over by the Government and used as an auxiliary hospital and a back-up to Catterick. George was transferred with me and finished up in the next bed to mine, right by the entrance door to this smaller ward in the mansion. Over the door there was a small balcony. You could imagine perhaps two or three people at the most being able to stand there, perhaps being able to play an instrument, perhaps an accordion, a violin even a cello, but not a piano. Whilst below on the parquetry wood blocked floor would assemble the dancers where now we had the beds.

Hauxwell Hall was open to all service personnel, Army, Air Force and Navy and in the building, there was so much talent I almost felt an ignoramus. George in the short time we were together became a great friend. There was also an Austrian Composer, a brilliant classical pianist. We had a commercial artist who carried with him a large scrapbook of his Army career. All in paintings and sketches of almost everything he had come across. We had a Sister in this mansion that was about twenty-four, in her bluish uniform, starched white collar and red cape, looked striking to say the least. So much so, that the commercial artist painted a coloured portrait of her in his scrapbook. This Sister was engaged to a Canadian Fighter Pilot and the moment he saw it, he asked if he would paint another in a larger fashion. He did so in oils and it almost breathed. It was alive and the pilot gave him fifty pounds for doing it. A princely sum in those days.

Another character was a political prisoner at one time, and he'd been imprisoned with a professor of mathematics who was also some sort of international chess player. Whilst in prison they must have played an awful lot of chess. Our chap, a Pole was so proficient he used to play the whole ward at the same time and win every time. He was phenomenal but was troubled with a very bad compound fracture of the leg which meant every ten to fourteen days the plaster had to be taken off and the leg dressed and re-plastered. I don't know what happened to him. He was still there when I left. Still in the same condition and fears for the possible need for amputation was constant.

At the far end of the ward was a man with the figure of Hercules just like some Greek or Roman statue. Sinews and muscle all perfectly shaped. One night we were all a bit boisterous, (remember our ages.) We were having a pillow fight the whole ward. Something was said by George and the Hercules chap strode down, lifted the bed with George in it and hung it on the balcony above the door. The bed was at least eighteen inches off the floor with George and his plastered leg, trying gamely to unhook the bed off the balcony when who walked in but the Matron. The Atom bomb wasn't known to us at that time but that night I thought I heard it go off as the Matron exploded. "You will all report to my office at 9 o'clock tomorrow morning."

Morning came and we lined up in the corridor by the Matron's office. Someone said, "She's coming." (Touch of Hollywood again.) George started singing *"Bless This House."* By the time Matron reached us we could see the path of tears running down her face. She turned to us waving her hands. "Get out all of you," and so we did.

We had the most wonderful concerts with the Austrian pianist and George. We heard every aria from every opera. We had our own Covent Garden in the lounge next to our ward. George was trained by Heddle Nash who in the thirties was considered to be Britain's greatest tenor, but I thought George was so much better. He sang like an Italian or Spanish tenor which no British singer did at the time. I asked him why he wasn't singing professionally. He said it was because his wife thought the theatre in any capacity was an uncertain means of earning a living. While there was an element of truth in that, it seemed tragic that a man with such a wonderful voice was prevented from using it for the benefit of those who might hear him sing.

One of my lasting memories is visiting the little family church that was located in the grounds. There was a euphonium in the church and George played the *"Lost Chord"* and sang as he played. It was and seemed, I think the closest I've ever been to heaven. Something that when I think about it, is recaptured and re-pictured in my mind and becomes more vivid the longer I dwell on it. George told me, before the war he often broadcasted with Toni and his Orchestra and sang with them in the Blackpool Pier concerts.

A lasting memory to this fine singer. I accompanied him to the Garrison Theatre at Catterick where he was invited to perform. The other artists were various ENSA (Entertainment National Service Artists) and suchlike personnel many of whom I think received a lifeline in their working life by being able to perform for the troops. These same people were often snooty and looked down on anyone they didn't know or hadn't heard of. Such was the attitude afforded to George and me. I remember vividly the looks on the faces of these individuals when this great voice began to sing.

When the plasters were taken off, we became the object and target of a lady masseur who whilst under treatment we collectively thought she was trying to break the limb again. She was slim, angular in build with only one object in mind, to get you fit and well again. I well remember the delight she showed when after many weeks of massage with no visible signs of improvement to a Grenadier Guardsman who was plastered from the neck down to the base of the spine and on this day she at last sensed movement in the lower part of his body and she exclaimed excitedly "At last we have hope" and she almost danced around the room. She was a spinsterish lady and very plain, but I think almost anyone in that room that day would have married her, for her joy told you so much we didn't previously know about her.

After leaving Hauxwell Hall with my plaster off I was moved to a rehabilitation centre at Queensbury near Halifax. What a centre that was with the finest physical trainers in the world. The Sergeant Major, a man of about forty, before the war a Physical Training Instructor in a Swedish Academy headed the group. He didn't appear to walk, he seemed to bounce. His gait was as straight as a die. His breathing no matter what exertion was unnoticeable. This applied to all. Dressed in black silk shorts which gleamed against the pure white vests on which in woven red silk was the physical training coat of arms. At other times covered with a fisherman's knit thick pure white sweater. The gymnasium was huge and had wall bars, not only around the walls but over the ceiling too. Frequently when we arrived for our specific treatments and exercises, they would already be there playing some form of tick, chasing each other all over the walls and across the ceiling, just like spiders racing about the place and then dropping down ready for action without a heavy breath between them. They were the supreme examples of fitness. At this centre they had devices and exercises for every type of break imaginable and I understand all modern techniques are based on what started at this centre.

On arrival we were examined by two doctors who then usually set you on a week one course, which consisted in my case with what was a fracture of the leg, having to jump small fences initially about six inches high, which increased in height and were moved closer together to quicken the movement. There were so many variations each specifically designed to improve and get you back to fitness. Each week you were examined by two doctors. They would then ask if you were satisfied with your progress. If you were and they were satisfied, they would move you on to the second week and so on. If you weren't, they would leave you in the same week but only the once. They were quite experienced in sussing out Plumbers Pendulum as it was called (swinging the lead.)

If all went well, you were A1 in six weeks. The final week consisted of Assault Course, ten mile runs and a final passing out test consisting of running from camp, up Queensbury mountain, along the top and down again, returning to the camp in twenty minutes., Personally, I was never so fit in my life as I was in the sixth week.

There was an airborne chap in the next bed to me. He came in after his parachute failed to open properly, resulting in him landing on a fence in the dropping zone and in doing so; he broke the wall of his stomach. The record for the mountain run was held by an athlete, who I was told played for the international Welsh rugby team before the war. I've got a feeling his name may have been Francis but I'm not sure. He was one of the physical trainers. His time was eleven minutes. The Airborne chap did it in twelve and so became the best of the intakes.

Finally, back to the wizard of the paint, the commercial artist. There was a huge canteen in the centre and this chap although only leaving Hauxwell Hall a few days before me, by the time I arrived he had covered one end of the wall with a mural. It was the River Thames at night, illuminated and included the Tower Bridge, it was so real I could almost see the ships moving. Too much viewing and I might have felt woozy. If it had been the sea especially the Irish Sea, I would have been sick. At the other end of the canteen he was in the process of completing and replicating looking through a skyscraper window in Manhattan. All the skyscrapers were visible, some shortening in height as they disappeared into the distance. Around the window were pink flowers, maybe roses, stretching themselves and twining around the frames. Again, you could feel slightly dizzy if you got too near, in case you fell out. The realism was that intense.

After passing out, I returned to Barnard Castle and resumed my training but with a new lot of chaps. It consisted of Drill, Wireless Procedure, Driving, Gunnery and general practice on the range and a touch of trench warfare. In the trench warfare I witnessed two incidents. As you will know trenches usually run straight a little way then bend at right angles; the reason being so that you can dodge round the bend in case anything goes wrong. It also means that if any explosion takes place in the straight run, you stand a better chance if you are located in the angle round the bend. In my case I was standing with the instructor as another rookie threw a hand grenade out of the trench, but unfortunately as he moved his arm back it hit the wall of the trench behind him and the grenade fell to the ground in the trench with us. As I told you before, I was quick earlier in this diatribe, but I was faster this time. All three of us were, lying in a heap on the floor but round the bend when the thing went off. Later a similar occurrence happened but this time the grenade was thrown out and hit one of the wooden stakes which carried barbed wire along the front of the trench. The grenade bounced back and landed at our feet. Once again, all speed records were broken, no one got hurt but lessons learnt.

Whilst all this was going on my mother back in Llandudno, who just twelve months before had lost her son George in the war and now had lost me to the Army, decided to join my father who was working and living in Stourbridge. She would be sixty-three years old at the time.

I left the 59th Training Regiment at Barnard Castle to join The Inns of Court Reconnaissance Regiment which was stationed in and around Newcastle-upon-Tyne. My squadron, A Squadron were billeted almost on top of one another in a drill hall in Newburn on the Scottswood Road featured in the old song of the same name. Arriving at a time that was rapidly approaching, D-Day, though we wouldn't know it until all Troop trades were allocated, so a Blitz Troop was formed. The idea being to follow a reconnaissance troop and to take over any retaliatory action that may be needed, whilst the reconnaissance vehicles quickly got out of the way, and of course, being available, to take over a position in a troop should a loss or vacancy occur.

When I arrived, I had contracted the skin infection Impetigo, which may have been caused by touching my face with oily hands whilst doing work on the vehicles. Irrespective of this I was immediately included in a four day training scheme, roughing it, sleeping in the open, very often wet, washing out of any available receptacle-not the best means of combating Impetigo, especially when after a day or two the towels became grey and grubby, but I was careful to use my own and tried to avoid touching the surface of the skin that was weeping to control spreading the infection.

On returning to the Unit I reported sick and was treated with a purple liquid, gentian violet which was dabbed on to the affected parts and quickly dried it up. Within three days I was cured thanks to the gentian violet and my well healing skin, but in those three days I was given the usual extra dose of duties which all newcomers get. Guard duties amongst them and I believe half of Newcastle turned out to see me after they'd heard of the violet spotted creature that was in Newburn.

We were packed like sardines in the Drill Hall. Our belongings mingled with each other's; we were so jammed. It didn't last long, no longer than a week or ten days which included the four-day scheme and the healing of the impetigo. We zoomed off to East Grinstead in Sussex. Billeted just outside the town in a lovely mansion in huge grounds, commandeered by the Government, with a lake at the rear. Unfortunately, there wasn't enough room in the building for all of us so Blitz, bivouacked in the grounds amongst the shrubbery. One who was in the same bivouac as me was a Scot called Jock, our vehicle driver. A man who would give his heart out of its socket if you needed it. Broad in dialect, lean in build, laconic with a sort of twisted grin, extremely blue eyes which with that grin lit up his features on so many occasions. He was also diligent and was more than careful to carry out the daily tasks that would ensure the vehicle would always be on the road and never break down.

At this stage I'd only been with the Regiment a matter of weeks and hardly knew anyone, even those in the troop to which I'd been allocated, Blitz Troop. It was necessary for me to visit the main building, the mansion, to inform or take something to the rest of the troop who were billeted in that building. I entered the room and was approached in a challenging manner by Ted an East End Londoner, who tried to take a rise out of me for no apparent reason and when I didn't budge, became a bit cocky and aggressive and finished up by saying "Right I'll see you tomorrow at 5 o'clock." I shrugged and said, "O.K. If that's what you want it's alright with me." Most of the troop was in that room as witnesses including the troop leader Corporal Alf.

The next day, well into the day, Ted searched me out and said, "I don't think we should be fighting over this as soon we may be fighting for our lives." I said, "O.K. If that's how you feel" and off he went. He was always a good friend thereafter and it proved to me more than ever as I've found out many times in my life, if you believe you're in the right then you seldom back down if ever. This man later was given compassionate leave due to his wife dying in childbirth. I spoke to him at the time expressing my condolence and sadness at his loss. He was about twenty-four at the time. Later the same day as he called off the fight Corporal Alf came around to our bivouac and when we were alone said "I liked what I saw yesterday. You're the sort that I want in my troop." This was from a man who I had only previously met once when I joined the troop and on saying his name I joked "Aye, I'm from Worcester myself" which was the home county where my parents were now living. I don't quite know why, but I think I may have upset him for he took my head in an arm lock and I could feel the pressure building until my head felt as if it was changing shape, then he released me. I guess I knew then what a walnut must be like in the jaws of a nutcracker. It was a show of strength and to show me who was boss. Apparently, this was a normal way with him and unfortunately for the other person there was no indication of this happening until he did it and then it was too late. Maybe with luck and with knowing it was going to happen, the result may have been different, but he was a formidable guy and I don't think I would have stood a chance.

Corporal. Alf was a broad Cockney who knew what he was doing, always and really knew no master - even the Officers would speak to him with care and respect. Indeed, Major, the Commanding Officer of the Squadron, swore by him for any arduous or super-human task and his bye-word in such instances was "Send for Corporal Alf."

The date now was towards the end of May 1944. The area was plastered with troops all gathered together deliberately for the date in June. As well as the variety of troops we also saw the many R.A.F. pilots and air crew who walked around, some with half faces, terribly contorted features, results of burning aircraft but all being helped by that foremost plastic surgeon later knighted for his services.

The Inns of Court consisted of four fighting squadrons A, B, C and D and Regimental Headquarters Squadron consisting of echelons. C Squadron was chosen to go over on D-Day. Casualties were expected to be in excess of ninety per cent. They weren't as it happened. They were much lighter. The other Squadrons followed some days later. During one of these waiting days I was standing by the bivouac in the evening air when this strange 'plane flew over making a noise like a loud two stroke engine with a tongue of flame issuing from the back. I thought at first it was some sort of small 'plane on fire, but suddenly the engine cut out and I watched it glide lower and lower into the distance, disappear and then heard the crump of the explosion. It was the first V1 rocket popularly known as the Doodle Bug.

We started out for Normandy about four in the morning and arrived at what turned out to be a sealed camp close to Tilbury Docks. We were held there until all arrangements were made with all the others who were going and for the ships at sea to be together to form the convoy which we were soon to be with on that journey to Normandy. As we approached the sealed camp we were greeted with little groups of women, mothers, sweethearts gathered at the corner of the street, 6 o'clock in the morning in their pinafores waving goodbye, some with tears rolling down their cheeks all with the stony faces of sorrow and dismay. We left Tilbury and joined a convoy and it took us four days to get to Normandy purely because of the numbers involved and the assembly of the convoy.

During that time, the sea was not my friend. I was never sick, but I had the vilest headache and I rarely touched food. My method later when I travelled from the Hook of Holland to Harwich was to bed down on the boat and to wake up hopefully in Harwich. Others seemed to be better at sea, couldn't care less, playing Crown and Anchor, daily, every hour for money, rapidly totting up over the four days until on the fourth, the prize money in the kitty was well over a hundred pounds and was won on the final day to loud uproar without any thoughts that the winner might never live to spend it.

As we approached Normandy, we took to our vehicles fully crewed, engine running, ready for action, waiting for the front of the landing craft to drop, for us to follow into the water. But first I must tell you of the amazing sight.

I looked around. I could hardly see the water for ships. There seemed to be thousands. Two battleships amongst them one of which, I think was the Rodney. They were both firing their huge naval guns alternatively, one after the other, firing at Caen, thirteen miles away. Huge flashes that lit up the whole sky followed by the crump and whoosh as the shells hurtled to the poor people in Caen. It was early evening and as each shell was fired so it became for one second, as light as day. We landed in the water at the right depth which was comforting. I'm not sure now what beach it was. C Squadron on D-Day landed on Juno beach with the Canadians so it could have been that one for us, but I remember it was mostly beach with green fields behind. I seem to have some recollection of a house or some similar building some distance away to the left. On the beach at one side were hundreds of kit bags all containing one of everything so that if you went into battle, were attacked and managed to come back there was something of everything waiting for you in the kit bag. All you needed then was another vehicle which could soon be provided.

There was also a huge marquee. At one end you stripped, threw your underclothes in a wire basket, proceeded at walking pace under a series of shower heads. At the end there were warm towels and a complete set of garments all; warm and aired. Oh! I forgot they also gave you some soap. The water was piped in from the sea, purified, warmed and came out in the shower. What organisation! I've always said since, if we could organise the peace as well as we did the war, we would be world leaders.

Reaching the beach, we were directed by the beach master to proceed in a certain direction which led us very soon into fields of green. I slept that night in a dried-up ditch. The next day wonder of wonders I received a parcel from the Pearson family (Grocers) in Llandudno. Inside was a fruit cake that was devoured almost immediately by a gusty lot of troopers. That same day the squadron were gathered in a field in the lay of a hillside and we were addressed by the Padre. I guess it was a blessing but more like a goodbye with what followed the next day.

The next day - shambles. The whole squadron advanced in single column, into a shallow valley along a track, through the fields, not a road. Roads were almost unknown in Normandy at that time. We had moved tentatively a fair distance, one troop behind the other, scout car, armoured car, armoured car, scout car, half-track vehicle (Blitz Troop) when suddenly the first Daimler armoured car was hit with an 88mm shell, then seconds later another Daimler further back. This meant that vehicles in between the two knocked out vehicles were trapped. We in Blitz Troop fired smoke so as to try to hide and disguise the position of the remaining vehicles and we hoped it would allow us to reverse back the way we'd come. Some vehicles reversed and others managed to turn around. We were able to do that because we had a tracked vehicle which was better than wheels in that terrain.

Assembling afterwards we found we'd lost two Daimler Armoured Cars. I can't remember any of the crews being lost but one of the drivers, weighing thirteen stones, actually got out of the armoured car, through the visor. The visor is an aperture not too large, through which the driver peers when he is driving. The size is just right to allow him to see enough and to afford him as much protection as is possible, but it was never meant to put a body through. The amazing thing is two days before the war ended the same driver did the same thing again, escaping without a scratch. It's strange how coincidences happen so frequently in life. Links and happenings which if you hadn't done one little thing, so many other things would not have happened.

For reconnaissance units or any forward troops, the worst possible trouble spots to look for, in no particular order are waterways, rivers, canals, bridges, valleys, crossroads especially if situated in country areas with perhaps sloping hills around. Anyone, especially in tanks or armoured cars will tell you the most feared gun in the last war was the 88mm. It was very accurate. It was versatile. Could be used as a field gun, featured on the Tiger Tank, was a mobile gun, could be towed anywhere and was also used by their navy. We had nothing to equal it at the time. It was deadly, accurate and one shell could go through the turret of an armoured car like a knife through butter. Explosive shells would pierce the turret then break up into dozens of razor-sharp red-hot pieces of metal, racing round the inside of the vehicle, severing and amputating everything in its way.

In Normandy the roads, such as they were, or the tracks, were lined with bushes and growth which went under the name of Bocage. We found out very quickly after our first lesson that the turrets on our armoured cars were visible to the watching enemy above the height of the Bocage and this is how they waited for us on that first disastrous morning. Their 88mm guns were on fixed sight, aimed on the track that we were travelling on and when the first vehicle got to that position, they had us. They'd seen us before we knew about them. They'd followed the turrets as we drove along the track. They didn't catch the first vehicle a Dingo Daimler scout car because it had no turret and was so low. So, what did we do later? We removed all the turrets off the armoured cars. Thus, lowering them and re-christening them SODS, (sawn off Daimlers.) By doing this we lost the 2-pounder gun but replaced it with a mounted Vicars K gun, one thousand rounds per minute. It didn't fire rat- a- tat- tat- tat but crackled, it was so rapid, and one bullet in five was a tracer which obviously helped to aim at a target, but unfortunately guided the enemy to your own position which didn't really matter to us as they already knew where we were. Later when we got out of Normandy, the turrets were replaced.

One of the tricks the enemy used were remarkable cut-outs of a Tiger Tank, full size, which could be situated, sort of hidden but deliberately arranged so that you would see it, stop in contact drill and in that second before you could reverse, you were hit by an 88mm shell fired from a position on the opposite side, their gun already positioned and aimed at the spot where they knew you would stop and in that second you were hit.

All Daimler Armoured Cars could travel as fast in reverse as in forward gears. The drivers in England rehearsed day in, day out practicing slalom in reverse, manoeuvring in and out of positioned oil drums on airfields and the speed they achieved, in reverse, was frightening.

Contact drill was both feet out (brakes and clutch) right hand on side of vehicle on pre-selector gear, pull back fully, two clicks forward (second gear) Left hand pull back on handbrake type lever into reverse, accelerate and away you go, backwards. The Armoured Car had a steering wheel in the back of the vehicle as well as the front. This allowed the Car Commander to steer and guide the vehicle. The Scout Car had a seat that was angled in such a way as to allow the driver to see easily behind him. The contact drill was the same for both vehicles.

After our first shambles of a performance we operated as single troops each working on a separate area, but all linked with wireless procedures. The Blitz troop I was in was generally attached to 4th troop. The eldest of my officers was a squadron leader Major, a Chartered Accountant in civilian life. He was twenty-five. My troop officer, very tall and suffered from Alopecia he was only eighteen years of age. Most crews were of that age. As a comforting gesture they told us our ammunition was the second-best quality. The first was given to the R.A.F; because of it being vital that there is no jamming of the guns when they are only allowed a split second to react in a dog-fight situation.

I am of the opinion that since that war I and many others in the Regiment only survived simply because the Germans were on their back foot. They were facing too much opposition, too much equipment, tanks, guns, aeroplanes, manpower. Had both sides been equal our casualties would have been more like those quoted for C Squadron on D-Day. They would have to be, as our constant job was to go out seeking the enemy and reporting back and this can hardly ever be done without the enemy first seeing you and taking the necessary action. So, in many ways I consider myself to be "dead" lucky.

On our first movement towards Caen I saw many of what I thought were tailors' dummies - Strange. They were waxen looking and very still. They were in fact German bodies and the realisation didn't strike fully home until we saw a Tiger Tank still smouldering looking like an old bedstead left out in all weathers. Closer inspection revealed in the tank a body that had been struggling to get out when the Typhoon rockets hit it. The breach block of the 88mm gun had been thrown back with the attack and had caught the chest cage of the crew member and had pushed his chest and ribs right up over his head like a corset. His intestines were already going green, putrefying and the flies were buzzing around. In the ditch alongside were two other members of the crew. The one was almost sitting up in the ditch, his eyes closed and one leg a shortened blackened stump. The other poor fellow was kneeling, his body somehow or other, upright, but his head, half of it was hinged back, held on by only an inch of scalp, bone or flesh. His head of hair hung right down to the ground by his buttocks. There was a total lack of blood in all cases. I saw a similar thing later in Holland.

We pursued our cause daily without many losses and watched from a distance as American bombers drenched an area with bombs. We could see in the sunlight the bombs dropping like silver fish and the cloud of dust and smoke, fog-like, rising from the target.

Our daily routine was exhausting, I suppose, but at eighteen or nineteen you don't really notice it. We had to go out early, as dawn was breaking, past our lines, past dug in troops and we returned just prior to dusk. It was June and the heat was pronounced. Each day on return we had to wash our hair to get rid of the greasiness caused by the heat, sweat and dust. We also had to restock all ammunition, petrol etc used on that day so that we were ready for anything.

In Normandy we had trouble in the early evenings when we returned to a safe haven for the night, by clouds of locusts, each three times the size of a bumble bee, which we called Buzzbees. They would crowd you out swarming around your head, knocking into you frequently causing most of us to wave our arms about and to run everywhere to try, unsuccessfully to outpace them.

On one of these evenings we returned about 9. o'clock and for ease and speed and probably from tiredness I decided to sleep under one of the echelon vehicles. I woke up at 4. o'clock in the morning at half-light and felt as though something was drilling into my brain via my left ear. I got up fast, banging my head on the underside of the vehicle as I did so, rushing, searching for a tap which I'd seen fastened against a post in the orchard.

I was conscious of one of our lads shouting "Halt who goes there?" I shouted, "It's me" and he recognised my voice and avoided shooting me. I put my head under the tap allowing the water to flood the ear and after a few minutes of dousing, the pain was lifted. The carburettor on the vehicle I was under had leaked and the petrol had dripped right into my ear, a thousand to one chance, inflaming the membrane. Fortunately, there was and have been no after-effects, though it has been said by my wife, years later, when perhaps I haven't heard her or mistakenly heard her. "You watch that ear the one you had the petrol in." They're marvellous, these women, these wives, these mothers.

Despite all this activity and the few hours of sleep, we were always provided with the means of having at least a weekly shower and change of clothing. So too, on one or two occasions we were entertained by a very small group from ENSA (Entertainments National Service Association) or Stars in Battledress. One time Terry Thomas, then an unknown entertainer with only two others for company, provided some real laughter in some barn on some farm in Normandy.

Another time we'd arrived back tired and dusty and were told a trio was performing for us that evening. There was a bit of a groan when we heard it was three women with a violin, cello and some other wind instrument but we went and sat there in dismay lulled by some insidious chamber music which when finished we decided to clap out of politeness. When the violinist bowed low, in thanks, and we could almost see her shoes, the clapping became thunderous and I could see the surprise, startled expression on the violinist's face. Being overjoyed she immediately bowed again, once more raising the roof with applause and shouts of encore. So, a disinterested affair suddenly became interesting and formed a topic of conversation for some time after. There was very little else to talk about.

Another time, operating with 4th troop we approached a largish village in Normandy called Vassey and because the road was impassable with debris, Blitz troop was ordered to investigate. Eight of us like shadows whisked through the village quietly without trouble and at the other end met the Americans who intended to do the same job but with a difference. Two hundred men all armed to the teeth fired shot after shot in every window of every building as they advanced. We followed them back to 4th troop watching in amazement.

As we advanced through France and passed village after village, we were often made a great fuss of. At Amiens we were held back for some reason and I with others was invited into a house where the large family sat around beaming and the mother proudly brought out a large bottle of olive oil which she'd been saving. She had a huge glass dish filled with lettuce, tomatoes and various other things and then with immense pleasure christened the lot by pouring on the olive oil. It was too much for me. I had a cigar instead and the old chap in the family demonstrated his hypnotic ability by practising on those French people who were present especially the kids. He pretended his thumb was a cigarette lighter and as he proffered it to an individual, so that person shrank away from it in case he got burnt.

I've suddenly thought I'm missing out something, the Falaise Pocket, which took place in Normandy and resulted in an enormous capture of German troops, but in our instance was a huge bluff. We were situated at the bottom of this bag-like bulge in which the Germans were trapped. We were there in case they came our way trying to escape the net that was closing around them. However, we were two men every five hundred or six hundred yards apart and had very little in the way of armaments to attack or defend ourselves with, just a few rifles, Sten guns and a Bren gun. Apart from this we had to stay there until the trap was successful. We managed the first twenty-four hours O.K. but during the second, sleep or the lack of it began to affect us. Each at different times would wake up with a start and then would walk down to wake the others who had also dozed off. Lack of sleep is still the most tortuous thing to bear.

It was here at Falaise I started to smoke to help lessen the awful smell from dead cattle that lay strewn around us. We lay watching and waiting in a gully and it seemed every time we had something to eat, the only breeze of the day would spring up and blow the aroma of the cattle on to us. Some cattle were still alive and wandering about in agony, they hadn't been milked for days so our

Scottish driver Jock, brought up on the Scottish Highlands milked as many as he could in the time we were there. He said the cows could hardly walk for the agony and the milk was more like porridge. It's remarkable how this touch of humanity can be seen even at the height of war.

We were allowed two days off after this stand-off at Falaise and we withdrew to park up in a field a few miles further back. When we got there, we debated for a moment or two on either having some food or having a kip. Whilst we were deciding the post arrived, being delivered by one of the lads in the echelons. Within a few minutes we were all asleep. Sometime later we woke up and prepared to eat and lo and behold the post-man arrived again. I said, "Forgot some mail, did you?" "What do you mean?" he replied, "Well you were only here not so long ago." "Oh aye," he said that was yesterday, and it was! The whole troop had slept non-stop for twenty-four hours, almost to the minute.

After Amiens and France, we entered Belgium meeting very little resistance and being feted as if we were royalty. Pears in their thousands were thrown into our vehicles, when standing; they were up to our waist. I never ate another pear for twenty years after Belgium. People hung onto our arms as we leaned over, they stormed the vehicles and crawled all over them. They were ecstatic, excited and beside themselves with joy. We were amongst the first into Antwerp and the streets were jammed with people, throbbing, exited, and delirious. One man reached and said in perfect English "Where do you come from, what part?" I replied, "Llandudno in North Wales." He then spoke to me in Welsh and I had to admit, almost with shame, "that although I lived there, I couldn't speak Welsh." He told me that he was president of The Old Welsh Society in Antwerp. I never cease to be amazed at these sorts of things that keep happening to me.

For the night, we moved out of Antwerp to a little suburb called Kontich. Our vehicles were located in a park. We were billeted in a dance hall sleeping on the floor. I decided to obtain the first copy of a newspaper that was being printed since liberation and was making my way to the building where they were being sold when I was ambushed and kidnapped by about a dozen young girls. They grabbed me joyously, they were drunk from liberation. They led me down some steps and into a cellar that was brightly lit, and music was playing. I was toasted and engulfed with cognac, fussed and I believe thrown about from one to another in what I supposed could be called dancing. I was never a dancer and I had army boots on, and I think I must have trodden on a few toes.

I eventually arrived back at the dance hall and one of the lads guided me into my bed space, me in reverse, by hand signals and occasional commands like "Right hand down, now left hand. Right, carry on. Straighten up. You're there." I had reversed into my space on hands and knees. The next day I was lying on my back under a vehicle when I was suddenly conscious of many pairs of feet all clad in women's shoes moving round and round the vehicle. I wriggled out, stood up and it was the girls from the night before. They were dancing around singing as they did so, "*I'm sorry. I'm sorry.*" They were happy, smiling, laughing and cheerful. I knew I had done no wrong. It seems I must have been treading on their toes and apologising and they were reminding me of it. They were nice, very nice, and very, very happy. Unfortunately, the Sergeant Major came on the scene. His first words were "What the devil have you got there a so-and-so harem. Get them out of here now," and so they dispersed waving and laughing. I never saw them again, but they remain vividly in my memory.

I was hugely impressed with the Belgium people. Their education standards were so high. So many people spoke so many languages. I knew one family and the daughter, eighteen years of age at Brussels University spoke five languages fluently. Whew! I felt like an ignoramus. This girl's best friend was the daughter of the Belgium Prime Minister, Messier Spaak, a friend of Churchill and like him in so many ways. I was certainly out of place.

This girl Yvette and her sole relative, her mother invited two members of our Squadron, to stay with them on a forty-eight hours pass, and I went with Peter (a brilliant pianist who couldn't read music but who could play anything once he'd heard it.) We had a lovely two days, visiting the theatre and being waited on hand and foot. During the course of our conversations Yvette mentioned that she had difficulty in obtaining English magazines or publications, so when I got back, I sent her some *"Lilliput"* and other similar magazines. I was invited again so I went and as I stepped into the hallway and the lift came down.   It stopped. Yvette stepped out, flung her arms around me and smothered me with kisses. Something I didn't expect and took me by surprise. We went to the theatre and I was generally made a fuss of and on my return to the Railway station she clung to me like a limpet. Letters were exchanged and in one of mine I mentioned that as the war was nearing its end, I'd been placed on the Z list, which meant that I was eligible to be transferred to the Far East, Japan, and Korea. I received a letter by return wherein she said she was intending to leave University and was seeking a nursing job in the Far East; it seemed obvious, to be with me. I was alarmed and I wrote back asking her not to do this, thinking I was unworthy of her, so well educated. (At this time, I knew of no one, back home who had been to University. It was the privilege of the wealthy.) Also, she only had her mother as family and I felt it unjust and impossible to cause her to leave her mother, who in all probability had given up much to provide her only child with the education she'd received. (I understood her father was a White Russian who was a Sea Captain who I think may have lost his life, for nothing, was known of him, by me.) Following my letter, I was due to visit Antwerp again on a forty-eight-hour pass and when I entered the flat, I was coolly escorted upstairs to and was curtly introduced to a young man who was a friend of Yvette's in University. From then on, I was practically ignored. We visited the theatre again, but all conversation was between them, not me. I left to return to the Regiment by thanking the mother, who never took her eyes off me

(I believe in sympathy with the treatment I'd been given) for providing me with the meals and the comfort which she lavished on me. I said Goodbye to Yvette and the young man briefly and I left never to return. I received a letter from Yvette a few weeks later wherein she hoped I would return safely to civilian life and wished me all the best for the future. I didn't reply. I had never been so demolished, completely ever before and for why? I couldn't really comprehend as I'd treated her correctly in every way. I never took advantage of her and I believe quite sincerely, at the time she was on a level far above my own and it would be invidious of me to steal her love and affection from everything and everyone, who up to that time had meant everything to her.

It was September, in Belgium; things seemed to have slowed down. I think we were taking stock, not wishing to go too fast as winter was approaching, in case we were caught short by a counterattack which did happen later, at Christmas in the Ardennes.

It was a Sunday morning the 10th of September 1944; Blitz troop was detailed to do a patrol. It was like a Spring morning, the soft sunlight and the fresh air invigorating and I think we may all have been daydreaming of other nicer things, when we made a left turn and hardly had we done so then a single shot rang out. Our heads instinctively touched the floor of the vehicle. Our driver reversed but a half track vehicle is no armoured car when it comes to reversing especially now we were under constant heavy machine gun fire. In reversing, our vehicle went between two trees and slewed half over, into a ditch pitching most of us out. The leaves from the trees were falling on us like confetti at a wedding being shredded by the gunfire which had now increased and was incessant. I could hear the bullets thudding into the trees. I could see some protruding from the trunk of the trees, and they were fizzing and bigger than normal rifle bullets. The bullets were dimensionally thicker, about three inches long and were phosphorus coated which meant; after they hit you, they would still burn inside you, which accounted for the fizzing. They were obviously equipped with a heavier type of machine gun and there was more than one. I only had a rifle which was virtually useless under the hail of bullets which we were receiving. Two brothers had snaffled the one Bren gun which they were operating together as a team. Eventually they needed more ammunition and Bob Bardrick climbed into the vehicle and threw down all the boxes we had. When he finished, he stood up ready to jump down. That mistake cost him his life for as he stood up a burst of bullets entered his body.

Directly in front of us from where the attack was coming was the Escaut Canal. We should have turned left before the one we did. It was a map reading error. At the front of the ditch we were in, there was a field of corn or something similar. We aimed the Bren gun at the crop and with one tracer bullet in five we hoped it would set the crop on fire and possibly rout the attackers. At this stage we didn't know the canal was the other side of the field and that's where they were attacking from. A comical side to this: there was a farmer working in the field and he never seemed to bother and carried on working. We escaped by crawling back along the ditch. We had already given Corporal Alf covering fire as he carried Bob on his back, out of the ditch and away to safety. Our lads, to my mind were careless in their evacuation, running across the raised section of the ditch, exposed to the gunfire, whereas me, no expert in infantry tactics, lay on the ground, my rifle held vertically between my knees, muzzle in my hands, ready for action and in that position rolled across the raised section actually quicker than they had ran and only one foot high or thereabouts, obviously a lesser target and ready to lie prone in a firing position at any given moment. Bob was taken to a Belgium doctor in Diest, the nearest town, who removed lengths of injured intestine and who we thought was taken back to England and was doing O.K.

However, since writing this, I have discovered Robert Frederick Bardrick died on the 12th September 1944, aged 33 and is buried in Leopoldsburg War Cemetery.

Because we were now certain of conquering Germany, requests were taking much longer and so it was with vehicles and for some weeks we moved around in a commandeered civilian Opel saloon car. We reached one town very near to a canal and as we were observing the area from the confines of a house overlooking the canal, we suddenly saw a slight movement which after watching silently, motionless for some time realised it was a German sniper who was perfectly camouflaged and had remained for the most part perfectly still. The Belgium agent wanted to shoot him straight away, but it was our job to observe and report back and despite being a sniper I couldn't kill anyone in cold blood in that meticulously callous manner, but then again, I hadn't had family gassed and murdered and so on.

As the winter drew near, we were well into Holland as well as Belgium and because of the inclement weather and the barrier of the River Rhine, advance more or less came to a halt. Instead we had a lot of standing patrols to do which meant leaving the vehicle behind and going on foot and sometimes at the last stage crawling on hands and knees and stomachs, usually to a forward trench that had been prepared under cover of darkness, with a cover over it for protection from the rain. Two persons were together on this duty, two hours on and four hours off. In the hours off we slept further back in a hay barn. I was about two feet off the roof, but I was as snug as a bug in a rug. The hay was so warm. One of the dangers was in crossing the open area or courtyard facing the trench. The enemy had two machine guns lined up on fixed sights which at haphazard times they would fire, and two streams of bullets would simultaneously sweep across this area, which meant that if you were crossing it at that moment, you'd have had it.

Another time we were drawn back into a town called Helmond, for a couple of days. My billet was in a house where I first saw the hand operated dynamo torch which needed no batteries. Whilst I was talking, three Messerschmitt 109's flew over, so low I could clearly see the pilot's faces. They didn't do anything. I think it was a token flight of defiance.

One job we had to do was to get rid of a tall building that we suspected in the daytime was being used as an Observation Post. Eight of us with four Jerry cans full of petrol, under cover of darkness were to cross the river in a little boat that was made available to us, and then we were to set fire to the building. At the last moment we were told that we had to have an officer with us. His name was Lieutenant Hill. He'd recently joined the regiment and he was given to us to "break him in" so to speak. In the end Corporal Alf reprimanded him in the pitch blackness for making so much noise. He asked the Corporal "if he knew who he was talking to." Corporal replied, "a so and so corpse and us with you if you don't keep quiet." He said afterwards "if that bloke lives through the war, he'll be bloody lucky." On the 30th March 1945 his words proved to be very prophetic. Lieutenant Hill died after his Armoured Car was attacked and lying in a ditch, with the loss of an arm he bled to death. But in all fairness, I couldn't say any fault lay with him.

After several weeks we returned to Belgium for what we thought was a couple of days rest. We stopped in a town called Malines or Mechelen (depending on the French or Flemish pronunciation) and Blitz troop was delighted to see a wrestling contest advertised in which they were asking for volunteer competitors. The moment Corporal Alf saw it; he put his name down for the contest the following evening.

Corporal Alf as a civilian, as well as working on the docks became quite a well-known local wrestler which explained our enthusiasm for the forthcoming bout. The next morning, we were called back to Germany and our greatest disappointment and Alf's was that he was robbed of his wrestling and we, our thoughts of missing that exhibition.

Just before Christmas we were called back into Belgium. It was reported that German Parachutists had been dropped near the Ardennes disguised as Americans and a lot of deaths had occurred from this deception. Then there was a major scare when the Germans pushed into the Ardennes and for a time it looked as though they were succeeding in their mission, so they called us back, but fortunately we were not needed and on the day we heard we were busy chopping logs for the huge stove that was in the house we'd taken over. We thought we'd be there for Christmas, but true to form we were moved before we had time to enjoy the burning of the logs. No doubt the people to whom the house belonged to would enjoy them later. We'd cut enough to last all winter.

Before I leave Belgium and Holland, I must tell you that at one stage in Holland we were camped out in an orchard amidst very red apples piled in great heaps. We were being targeted all day by "moaning minnies," fifteen barrelled mortars, firing simultaneously all landing indiscriminately all over the place which made them even more dangerous and yet despite this, the frequency of it made you become careless and contemptuous. Earlier I wrote about the shock to the body and in those cases the absence of blood. I mentioned another example as being in Holland. This is the one I was thinking about.

One chap, not from our unit was walking across the orchard when these mortars were falling and suddenly as he was walking his right arm disappeared and in its place was strings of flesh, hanging where his arm had previously been. For some seconds that man didn't realise the shrapnel had torn his arm off. It seemed as though the suddenness had shocked everything into a numbness that prevented him knowing.

When the winter was fading and things were gearing up ready for the charge into Germany we still couldn't do much in our proper role, we had to cross the Rhine first and until this happened we were utilized as traffic control, guiding all the heavy stuff that was coming up ready for the crossing, tanks, field guns and such like. It was whilst I was standing at the side of the road fulfilling that duty, in a quiet moment; no traffic at all, that Winston Churchill came by. I'd seen him previously in Normandy before Caen fell, but this was different, more personal, I was the only one in sight, most unusual. Mortars were falling but he was poised in the turret of a Daimler Armoured car (our type of vehicle) fully visible from the chest up, a cushion fixed on the turret on which he could rest his elbows, dressed in khaki army uniform, a sort of sombrero on his head, cigar in his mouth, half grin on his face and two fingers aimed at me in his victory salutation. I was barely four feet away from him. The only protection he had was a jeep in front and one behind, both with mounted Vickers K guns with two military police in each vehicle.

I turned with excitement, the adrenalin surging, leaping a ditch which normally I would have landed in the middle of. I rushed into the bivouac shouting "I've just seen Churchill." "Don't be so and so daft" was the reply and by the time they'd got out, of course he'd vanished.

It was possibly in this period but prior to it, that we were in a barracks at, I think, Fallinbostel for a few days and I was given two displaced persons, Lithuanians to help me with various jobs. They were in their late twenties but looked middle aged because their skin was yellowish and heavily lined. I felt this was probably due to the harsh conditions of the country they came from, but they were tremendously strong and would carry two Wireless Set No.19 batteries, one under each arm, measuring approximately two feet long by 12 inches wide by 18 inches deep and run up the steps with them, whereas I could manage only one, with both arms, with difficulty. I used to offer them a cigarette whenever I had one and they bowed in courtesy and thanks with a certain look of disbelief or amazement in their eyes as they did so.

One day when we'd worked for some time with no cigarettes being offered because I had none, the eldest of the two signalled with his hands and I returned the signal with a shrug and a wave of my arms indicating I'd got none, whereupon with a huge smile on his face he opened the flap on his chest pocket and pointed to two cigarettes and offered me one. I realised then, how all nationalities can be much of a muchness and enriched by this knowledge and what these two men had endured. Taken away from their families and never having seen them for years and through no fault of their own had become displaced persons, without anything or anyone. It gave me food for thought.

When they learnt that my regiment was moving on, they asked me more by sign language than speech what my initials were and the day before I left, they presented me with a ring made out of a German silver mark piece with my initials raised on the surface. They'd fashioned this with hardly any tools to work with and I was immensely proud and pleased to receive it and as they shook my hand, I was aware of the fluid (tears) that appeared in their eyes. That ring disappeared after the war, when we were stationed at Leck. I still feel that loss.

At last we crossed the Rhine, this was innovative to say the least, the Royal Engineers with tremendous speed placed pontoons, which were, in effect blown up rubber dinghies, side by side and then on top of these they rolled out two metallised tracks the exact width of the vehicles that were about to use the crossing including tanks, even bearing their weight.

As we crossed in our half-track vehicle I stood up and held a camera vertically above my head and as we reached the other side and started to move up the sloped banks, I clicked the shutter and months later when we were in, Leck, Schleswig-Holstein this photograph won me first prize in the interest section of the competition. It actually showed a long line of vehicles one behind the other crossing that floating roadway with nothing but water between both widths of wheelbase. A few bullets directed at the blown-up rubber dinghies and the whole lot would have been disaster.

After crossing the Rhine near Wesel, we entered Germany through a road that was cut overnight through the Reichswald Forest. There must have been several hundred Royal Engineers who felled the trees which were then laid side by side on the ground, levelled by huge bulldozers which created a roadway through the forest, hidden by the trees, through which, tanks, artillery and we entered Germany. A tremendous feat well in keeping with the likes of Brunel and Thomas Telford.

Our first stop and contact with a German family was when we entered a house, looking for some sort of pan in which to fry eggs (which Corporal. Alf had obtained from somewhere or other) the family were dumbstruck, silent, and afraid. The two teenage daughters stood terrified; trembling obviously thinking something terrible was going to happen to them. They couldn't speak, they couldn't move. It seemed to me as an onlooker that they been indoctrinated with the most obvious adverse propaganda.

Soon after, in a suburban area, our vehicle and fourth troop were halted, waiting for orders to proceed. In the field alongside were a number of German workers who stopped and looked silently at us. For some reason or other one of the armoured car operatives decided to rotate the turret and the two pounder gun moved round in the direction of the workers, in the field and as it moved pointing in their direction I saw the look that transposed their features from curiosity to fear, some started running to the side, others dropped to the ground, some of them gripping the persons next to them in protection and then as the turret moved back to its original forward position, the almost disbelieving relief as they realised they were not going to be massacred. I guess the operator was merely checking on the function of the gun for he wasn't even aware of what I'd seen.

Entering Germany our real job began again in earnest and this time it was on German soil so was likely to be more difficult. I suppose it was, but they were on their back foot and they must have known they were losing. The ordinary man and woman, I think, did, but the fanatics, the S.S; the Camp Commanders and so on fought to the bitter end.

As soon as we entered a village, town or area and there was no visible signs of the enemy our practice was to get hold of the Burgomaster (the equivalent of our Mayor or Local Chief Executive) who would then be questioned in no uncertain manner by our Squadron Interpreter, who was a naturalised German or Austrian Jew whose family had been wiped out by the Nazis. He learnt whilst he was with us that his mother and father were both gassed a few weeks before the war ended. You may imagine what an interrogation was like by the man, but you'd have no idea. Mercy was an unknown word. The moment he spoke saw the persons face blanch, in horror, trembling, tears every emotion of that kind, and appeared in seconds. God knows what he was saying to them, but we grasped some meaning when he handed them a spade and they started digging their own grave. Usually this did the trick and they babbled everything they knew in total terror and submission.

One exception was a young boy of sixteen who wore German uniform and wore the Iron Cross in two orders, first and second class. I believe they were earned on the Russian front. He spoke faultless English and replied in English to everything said in German. He appeared to be fearless. Totally cool and collected. Arrogant and was thoroughly brainwashed in Nazi theology. He said he was making his way to Hamburg where a pocket of fighting was still going on. He said his life was dedicated to the Führer and that should he escape, which he intended to, he would make his way to Hamburg to fight for the glory of the Reich, the Fatherland. After fruitless questioning the Interpreter threw him a shovel. He took his tunic off and as a rough wooden cross was fashioned for authenticity, he dug like someone on a bonus. Everyone was taken aback, and the troop officer said "Take Sten guns. I'll line you up and give you the opening orders but will not give you the order to fire." When the lad had finished digging, he calmly put on his tunic and stood at the head of the grave. Fourth troop lined up and the opening orders were given and then suddenly in a loud voice "Fire." Some did then others followed. The lad had given the firing order himself and he fell, his chest pumping blood. He said one word. "Please." The troop officer shot him, he had to. This episode not only shocked those present. It transfixed them and they were subject to the memory of it for a long, long time. Some if still living, probably still are. My belief is that the young lad really thought he was going to be shot and under no circumstances would he allow us to give that firing order.

This method of interrogation happened in every town we entered, all with the same effect. I saw crack S.S. Panzer Division men buckle at the knees when the Interpreter spoke to them. Three of them wept in a huddle in one instance. All that they could say was "Rakete, Rakete" and wave their hands in the air. They were referring to a Typhoon attack which had destroyed their Tiger Tank, but fortunately for them they'd got out and ran away as far from the tank as they could before the attack which saved their lives but affected their mentality.

It was 11 o'clock at night and we'd halted against a hedge which ran alongside the roadside. My troop officer had been called to an intelligence meeting where he was informed and told us that this place known as Belsen was liable to suffer from an outbreak of Typhus and on no account must we leave the vehicles.

I didn't see anything of Belsen but Bert the driver of the squadron water tanker, was called upon to supply the camp with water and when he returned, he was ashen faced and said he'd never seen anything like it. Corpses, shrunken, skeleton like, shovelled into pits and buried, others too weak to walk, too weak to smile, too weak to rejoice at their release from starvation, torture and human degradation.

We were the first troops into Lüneburg, where eventually the surrender treaty was signed. This was an area similar to Salisbury

Plain and General Montgomery expected that if there was going to be a setback, this is where it was likely to happen as it was great tank battle countryside.

We entered it quietly without a shot being fired and discovered the Germans had declared it an open town. I don't know why though I suspect they were worse off than we thought. There was a large hospital there full of injured troops. Maybe they were thinking of them.

General Montgomery was delighted and sent every man in the squadron two bottles of champagne. I'd never drunk champagne before and I considered it to be some sort of funny 'pop.' I did however sleep well that night. When we left Lüneburg, (after handing over to the S.A.S the next day). The General was waiting at the side of the road in his staff car. He stood up and saluted every vehicle as we passed him by. Quite a feather in our cap.

We moved on. The Russians were moving too. To the dismay of our political leaders who knew the Russians were going to reach Berlin before us, or the Americans and that was the last thing they wanted, we were told at all costs to get to Schleswig-Holstein and the Danish border before the Russians. We shot like an arrow non-stop across Germany reaching the Danish border and settling in a village called Leck a few miles from Flensburg. Blitz troop was billeted in the Burgomaster's house on the main road entering the village. There was our equivalent of a pub opposite and a village square close by where our squadron vehicles were parked. It was whilst we were here that the war ended on Tuesday the 8th of May 1945 and there was an immediate ban on speaking to Germans, called non-fraternisation.

Denmark was just down the road and with the surrender some thousands of German troops who had been stationed in Denmark, many of them either old or young, some recovering in convalescence, all fully armed and carrying all their possessions with them. As they marched past, we could hear them singing military songs two or three miles away as they passed pushing old prams or anything that could carry their belongings.

I was standing at the gate watching them when the wheel of one of the prams came off and two or three of the men started to repair it. At the same time the Burgomaster's daughter spoke to me at the gate. I couldn't understand her and had to be careful because of the non-fraternisation order. One of the German soldiers looked up and said in perfect English, but with an American accent. "She wants to go into the loft to collect some of her belongings." I waved her in and said to the soldier. "Where did you learn to speak English like that?" He grimaced and said. "I was an aircraft designer for Messerschmitt," but in the 1920's he went to America and joined one of the big aircraft firms. After Hitler came to power in 1933, he started receiving overtures to return to Germany. Finally, after increasing his financial terms, he received an offer he couldn't refuse and returned to Germany. "Worst mistake I ever made," he said ruefully. He'd only been called up during the last six months because his work was of national importance. He spoke English in the same way as we do, colloquially, but with an American accent.

Within a few hours of arriving in Leck several of us had to move to the next village, Niebüll where there was an airfield. The hangars were crammed with jet aircraft. We were only there long enough to see what we saw, when we were bundled out by military police who placed an embargo and armed guard on the whole of the airfield. Next day huge American Transport planes landed. The jets were dismantled, put into wooden crates, loaded on the planes and whisked off to America for inspection and examination.

In the village of Leck we had our squadron barber's shop. One day we couldn't get in and on forcing the door we discovered his body inside. It was said that his wife had gone off with an American. Though different, another casualty of war. It was March and the ground was frozen solid and I was chosen as one of the coffin bearers. We travelled a fair distance to a churchyard where the grave was supposed to be ready. When we arrived, there was no grave dug. We had to do it. The ground was like concrete and we were all in our best battledress etc. The Padre, not ours, acted as though he wanted to go home. It was the poorest mumble of a graveside oration I've ever witnessed. I left with less of a religious fervour

Also, in Leck I was invited to a play, *"Candida"* by George Bernard Shaw performed in German and seemed to be thoroughly enjoyed. The people in this village though understandably reticent at first, appeared to me at the time to be the most like ourselves, often showing an easy and friendly attitude towards us, a facsimile of ourselves including the humour which we are supposed to be famous for. I wondered, being so close to the Danish border whether they were less influenced by Nazism and had more of a leaning towards the Danish. We certainly had no trouble at all with them and the children almost loved us, they always wanted to be with us and when we left several stood at the roadside wiping tears from their eyes.

I also won a photograph competition in the "Interest" section, taken whilst crossing the River Rhine and I was fortunate to be allowed to use a dark room in a commandeered German residence which was enormous and equipped on a scale second to none. It not only had the normal vertical enlargers but also had horizontal ones which were able to produce prints something like six feet square on a frame on the wall at the far end of the room. I did this a few times for one and the other. Some days I was in there from morning 'til night.

At Leck we were encouraged in all sorts of directions, sport, photography, record playing sessions, horse riding etc. I became a leading light in five a side hockey on a pitch that was boarded all round so that the ball never went out of play. Our troop, Blitz troop won the inter troop competition also against the officers, who contained an Oxford Blue on their side, and we beat them.

It wasn't so much that I knew all about the ins and outs of hockey, it was simply that I'd got a good eye for distance, power and movement. I was chosen on one occasion for the Regimental team which was represented by the Oxford Blue and several regular non-commissioned officers who had served for many years pre-war in India, the home of some of the greatest hockey players in the world. One member in particular who could run the length of the pitch with the ball either balanced on the flat blade of the hockey stick or could bounce the ball up and down on the flat blade of the hockey stick and then nearing the oppositions goal would allow the ball to drop to the ground and then hit it like a bullet usually in the back of the net. No one in the team, contrary to most players raised their hockey stick above waist height. The power of the stroke was created by wrist action. This Regimental team was never beaten and on being challenged by the unbeaten American Army Group, succeeded in beating them by two clear goals.

Being so close to the Danish Border we managed to cross and were able to indulge in eating the most wonderful sponge cake, served with a large jug of fresh cream, all for two or three cigarettes. We were able to buy Slazenger badminton rackets, again for a few cigarettes. I was also fairly proficient at badminton and was entered for the British Army Championships. The organizer being a certain P.T Sergeant Instructor who'd been posted to our regiment and who had betted against me way back in England at Barnard Castle and once again he proved himself useless by being too late in registering my name as a competitor, so I missed out.

Post War

When the war ended an immediate problem was Law and Order and to sustain this, each Regiment that was in occupation of a certain town was given the job of carrying this out. It generally meant that the Commanding Officer and his second in command became judges of the Local Law Courts on alternate days. In our case, a Major a law student in civilian life became the judge and arbiter. On the alternate days, Captain his second in command acted in that capacity. Though I believe in civilian life he'd been in the insurance business.

One of the first jobs given to our troop officer was to visit three displaced persons camps and after doing so he returned violently sick from the smell and state of the camps where all the inmates for the most part lay on their beds rotting. These camps were actually decent camps if they were kept in order and they were occupied by all nationalities including Russian, Rumanian, Lithuanian and Polish all of whom suffered from inertia caused by fatigue. In those three camps there was over six thousand people and the Major's first words on hearing what the Lieutenant had to say was "Send for Corporal Alf" and so Blitz Troop went. The inmates were billeted in wooden huts with an entrance door at one end, followed by a room with four double-decker bunks in it containing eight men, then a walled partition with a central door followed by another room with the same number of double-decker bunks in it. A third room followed, this time with a central exit door at the end. We entered the hut through the appropriate door, Corporal Alf leading. "Right! Up you get." Eight heads barely lifted as they lay back on their bunks. He carried on through the other two rooms with the same reaction, but then returned to the entrance door this time standing between each set of bunks wrapping his arms around them then heaving leaving the occupants on the floor. Eight men in each room and so he continued right through the camp. At one stage several of them waited for him as he came out of the hut and each was flattened with a forearm smash, head butt or a kick in the vitals. Within the hour the camp was a hive of activity, men filling in old latrines and digging new ones, burning lice-laden straw and eventually lining up, all 2,000 to be treated in the hair and down their trousers with DDT, (Dichlorodiphenyltrichloroethane) which had just been discovered and was ladled onto them with spatulas the size of a child's sea side sand spade. Later the same numbers were filed into the showers, which were green with non-use though the equipment was good but had hardly ever been used. Some had ankles like bad apples, cankered and rotten with festering sores but too idle to do anything about it. This procedure was carried out on all three camps.

Days later when the camps had settled down and the inmates were able to wash, clean and look after things they used to venture into the village and for a couple of cigarettes they would lay under the vehicles and clean them until they sparkled. Most were illiterate, most had seen little of modern times, some having never seen a train and I remember when one of the lads opened a tin of what during the war was classed as iron rations only to be used in an emergency, but now being peacetime, that rule was relaxed. The tin contained a chocolate drink produced by Cadbury's and Fry's with I.C.I. providing the chemical element in the bottom of the tin which had a small lid which could be levered off, then the burning end of a cigarette would be applied to the element and within two minutes the contents would be boiling hot chocolate. When they saw this there was a babble of talk and a huge movement by them to see more of this magic which I'm convinced they thought it was.

At other times Corporal Alf was known to have pulled vehicles out of mud laden ditches on his own. His civilian job was on the docks in London working for Tate & Lyle, unloading two hundredweight bags of sugar. He reckoned he used to carry one under each arm, up the steps and then store them in the warehouse. This was constant. He was as strong as an ox. Worth his weight in gold to the Army.

In the autumn we moved to a sea plane base at Tönning, a bit too near the Baltic Sea for me. We were there at Christmas. It was freezing and there were huge blocks of ice floating in the sea. At 2 o' clock in the morning I had one of the finest meals I've ever had in my life. We were on patrol along ours and the Russian border and we called in a little bakery. Brown bread rolls were just coming out of the oven. They were still hot, and we were given some substitute fat in place of butter or margarine to spread on them. It was freezing and I've never tasted anything so good. In memory I can almost taste them again.

It was at Tönning in this huge seaplane base, in one of the hangars, that one of the Daimler Armoured cars, with the Vickers K Machine gun mounted on the top of the turret, was being guided into the maintenance area, the entrance of which was circular and unfortunately the chap guiding it in, failed to notice that the arch of the circle was too low and the barrel of the K Gun had bent totally backwards as it was driven slowly up against the steel and concrete construction. The squaddies who were witnesses were doubled up with laughter and various comments were made including "Don't touch the trigger or you'll shoot yourself," amidst roars of laughter. Such is the baseness of humour with servicemen and often when it is to the distress of others, but there is never real harm or malice in it. When I was demobbed, the Court Martial for this offence was still due to take place.

Later we moved back into the heart of Germany. We stopped at one barracks; it may have been Fallingbostel. I'm not sure, but each evening there was a firing squad in action at the far end of the barracks, well out of sight. I don't know much about the sentencing of those who were about to be shot, but I understood they were for the most vicious of crimes. One I know was shot because he was responsible for carrying out tests on babies including the injection of benzene in the baby's veins. Another one at night directed four Americans in a jeep to use the Autobahn instead of the poorly conditioned roads. They did and, in the dark, finished up by driving off the end of the uncompleted Autobahn with a colossal drop involved.   All were killed.

Volunteers for the firing squad were sometimes asked for.   The system seemed to be that the person to be shot was blindfolded and tied around his middle to a solid wooden post. I understood one Polish fellow who had committed some hideous crime kept on moving around the post for quite some time causing as much trouble as he could. He didn't like the idea of being shot.

When we were close to Braunschweig, I was allowed to visit a Police Station and was led down a passage to the end where there was a rising step, the space being covered by a curtain. The person showing me around, held me back, pulled back the curtain and I was looking into an all-white tiled room with sloping floor to a central drain. At the front directly behind the drawn back- curtain was a guillotine. The blade very heavy and gnarled, no sharp edge, not needed, the weight of the blade does the trick. As soon as the victim trips over the raised step, falls through the curtain, the guillotine operates and the moment the head is severed, water jets spurt all over the tiled walls washing and dispersing the blood. I was surprised at this being in Germany. Another thought I had was just a month or so earlier and that chap that showed me the guillotine might well have pushed me through the curtain.

At some barracks or other where we hung out for a couple of days and I didn't know what to do with myself, I obtained a square wooden board and fixed on it four 1,000 or 2,000 watt bulbs, massive they were, then walked into the hut where all the lads were either reading, yapping or writing letters home, plugged the board into the power point, switched it on and whoosh, a huge flash of light followed immediately by pitch blackness as all the lights were fused. There were a few exclamations and blokes staggering around in the dark their arms either outstretched trying to feel their way around or with their hands over their eyes. "What the hell have you done?" was one exclamation. It was then I discovered the modern method of re-fusing the lights without fuse wire by pressing a button switch - so easy - so advanced. Nothing like it seen before. Light years ahead of us at the time. (Excuse the pun.)

For some time, we were stationed in a very up to date German barracks in Wolfenbüttel, Wolfsburg near the Volkswagen factory being nearby. This was the company that was offered to every

British and American car manufacturer as reparations from the war. No one wanted it so a British Army Major with no motor manufacturing experience whatsoever was detailed to do something about it. He revolutionised the company and set it on the lines it is today. In that factory there is a plaque dedicated to this man that was placed there by the employees in grateful thanks. Funny thing wars, strange conclusions sometimes.

The Sergeants Mess at Wolfenbüttel, was the best I've ever been in. The food was excellent and prepared in beautiful organized kitchens. The Mess itself was carpeted. The tables were arranged as in a restaurant with pure white tablecloths on them. The meal was silver service at its best. The room itself was lengthy with windows all down one side, at the end walls too, providing a wonderful area of light and comfort.

At Wolfenbüttel, there was a lovely theatre and outside in front of it there was a lake which in the winter became a popular skating arena. It was in this theatre that I saw the young Elisabeth Schwarzkopf, before she became a world renowned soprano and at the end as she was presented with a bouquet the whole audience joined arms and as the music played each theatre row swayed alternatively until the whole audience was rhythmically moving side to side. Quite a moving experience. I wondered how it was, that people who could enjoy this music then link arms and sway from side to side, obviously with no thoughts of war, of bombing, or anything like that, could make war.

Another time in the packed theatre there was one empty seat along-side mine. A soldier made his way along the row. I looked up. "Hello Queki," I said. "Hello Norm," he replied. He was a school friend from the same school I attended in Llandudno. We spoke to each other just as if we knew we were going to meet. It is since, I've thought more about it. What a coincidence.

One day at Wolfenbüttel I was late entering the Mess and was still finishing my meal alone, when I saw a German woman who was employed as a general help in both the Sergeants and Officers Mess sitting at the far end of the room with her back towards me. I was aware of her shoulders shaking and I realised she was crying. I asked her, "What was the matter?" "Ich bin so freude," she said, "I am so happy" and after further questioning this is what she told me.

Apparently, she had lived in Berlin and the Russians in the taking of that city showed no restraint or mercy and were using field guns, used normally for long range, at the end of her street destroying house after, house after house. She and the others fled for their lives but were soon overtaken and captured by the Russian soldiers who looked for the nearest place to take them. It was in a bombed outbuilding that she was raped many, many times by one after the other. Finally, she was discarded and collapsed in a heap whilst they paid attention to new captives one of which was a young woman with a baby in her arms. She was grabbed and ordered to undress. When she shook her head, the soldier grabbed her baby and holding it upside down by the ankles signalled her again to undress. This time she did and as the soldier moved towards her, he dropped the baby headfirst on to the floor. The mother screamed and lurched towards the soldier aiming a pin taken out of her hair. The soldier parried her movement and with one stroke with a large knife whipped out of his belt drew it across her throat. She dropped to the floor dying. The woman telling me this rose to her feet in anguish and the same soldier grabbed the front of her dress pulling her to her feet and went to repeat the motion with the knife when someone, she believes an officer, called from the doorway. The soldier immediately let her drop to the floor then left the room. Another second and she'd have been dead.

She eventually returned to the remains of her house, searched for food and old clothing. Finally wrapping the food around her body, dressed in old black dark clothes she started walking from Berlin into the surrounding countryside, posing and looking and dressed like an old woman. It took her several weeks, living off crops which she collected from the farmer's fields. Sometimes she was helped with odd bits of food by the farmers. In time she reached the border separating the Russian Zone from the British and crossed it in a wild unmanned area in the middle of the night. She worked in whatever capacity she could until she reached Wolfenbüttel where she managed to be able to work as a civilian help in the Messes. In exchange for which she received some kind of remuneration, but better still in her own words, three meals a day and a room of her own in which to live and also medical attention from our own Doctors. This was the reason for her happiness and the tears. She'd just been informed that she had contracted no venereal disease of any kind and of course she already knew she wasn't pregnant, so the tears were of happiness without doubt. That woman's look is another that will always remain in my memory. She believed her husband had been killed in Stalingrad. Is it not so often the wrong people pay the price in war?

Then we moved to Helmstedt and we had a new Major commanding the squadron, a Major who like the proverbial new brush wanted to sweep clean. I was running a training cadre at the time. With the war finished and demobilisation taking place I was made up to Sergeant and was the Squadron Signals Sergeant with a Signals Officer above me. One day I was in the training classroom talking to an old friend from fourth troop, the troop we'd been most attached to during the war. Phillip was his name. He was college educated and never particularly appeared to hurry either in speech or action. Major entered the room and I pulled up to attention and saluted and so did Phillip after a fashion, but much slower and belatedly and sloppier. I saw the Major's face look with scorn at Phillip with his crumpled battle dress, his hair which was that short stuff that never looks tidy. The Major left the room but I felt that Phillip was a marked man and so it turned out to be.

Some weeks later when we were on a grassy plain doing a gunnery exercise, under the eyes of the Major, who should turn up but Phillip, who the day the war finished announced to all and sundry. "No more soldiering for me. That's me finished." He promptly got a job in the echelons bringing in the supplies etc and having no more duties, parades, guards and suchlike to perform, but then the eagle eye of the Major spotted him. "You," he said. "Come here. What's your trade?" "Gunner/Op sir," Phillip replied, handing him one of his so-called salutes. "You can have a go." "Yes sir, may I go in the kitty sir?" "By God you will," the Major retorted.

I must stop here now and tell you about Phillip and his car commander Sergeant Jim a Scot who won the M.M. (Military Medal) for picking up mines with his bare hands and stacking them tidily out of the way until one went off the other side of the track and injured his ankle and put him in hospital for six or eight weeks but he returned and he and Phillip were a team the like of which you've never seen.

This was in Germany whilst the war was still on. Fourth troop and we, Blitz troop had made a contact. We'd reversed out of trouble around a bend in the road which hid us from our contact a Lieutenant, nineteen years of age decided he wanted to go on foot, alone around the bend to see what he could see, but a bit of an argument ensued between him and Sergeant Jim, but the officer pulled rank on him and off he went with a pistol in his hand and grenades attached to his belt. Meanwhile we lined up ready to go after him at a moment's notice. We watched him disappear using the roadside ditch as cover. Hardly had he disappeared when we heard sound of firing followed by a dull crump. We raced after him in formation. Scout car, armoured car, armoured car, Scout car and Blitz troop in a halftrack vehicle. As we turned the bend, we saw a green beret thrown up into the air from the ditch which told us where the officer was. As we sped along the rural road, a German soldier stood up in the ditch with a bazooka at his shoulder. As he fired Phillip beat him by a split second, with the two pounder and the German soldier vanished, vaporised. The bazooka shot hit a tree behind the armoured car, exploded and threw shrapnel all over the place. Phillip manoeuvred the gun pointed at the door of the house that the German soldiers were running into. His first shot hit the window at the side of the door. All his next shots followed the Germans through the door after them. This was done whilst the vehicle was travelling. It was enough to turn the vehicle over because of the repercussion each time the 2-pounder was fired. We returned through the village with no sign of the enemy. We picked our officer up on the way back. Apparently, a German soldier had stepped out of the ditch fired at our officer which was the shots we'd heard, and the officer had then thrown a hand grenade at him which was the crump we'd heard. Our Officer however had lost part of his thumb in the exchange of fire. Phillip stepped out of the vehicle looked around in his usual calm slow manner and had a gentle moan that his kettle and teapot which was fastened to the outside of his vehicle was now full of holes from the shrapnel caused by the bazooka.

Such was the man who the Major thought he could make an example of. By now the crews of the other vehicles knew that Phillip was back, and they quietly gathered round. No one wanted to miss this. Oh! Yes, and the Major agreed that Sergeant Jim would crew for him. I think everyone stole a grin at each other. Together they were like an oiled machine. Phillip climbed into the gunner's seat, his eye quickly fixed to the telescope, nuzzling and feeling the weight of his old friend. Sergeant Jim was in position, one shell already in the spout. The Major was standing on top of the car holding the turret. Well, he was for the moment until he gave Sergeant Jim instructions to fire at will, which he did. First shot to the right of target. "Shall I carry on sir?" "You might as well," said the Major. Jim said, "Rapid fire," and his arm moved. Bang, bang, bang, shell after shell with hardly a second between. The armoured car bucking all over the place. The Major already thrown to the ground, his face reddening as he saw plume after plume rising from the tank in the distance, the size of a matchbox, after shell after shell went into the middle of it. Then silence as the exercise was over and Phillip emerged the same calm unimpressive looking soldier, eyes now searching for the kitty which was already being pushed at him. That episode recurs time and time again in my memory.

Before I leave Phillip and Sergeant Jim, I must tell you of an incident in Normandy when Sergeant Jim was separated from the rest of his troop and he ran headfirst into a contact with a Tiger Tank. The 88 mm gun of the Tiger Tank was in the quarter of an hour position, offset from pointing at Jim and his scout car, which he was commanding at the time. We heard him shout "Stop" to his driver over the radio then "Stop still" and the vehicle stood stock still, whilst the crew of the Tiger Tank were feverishly turning the huge turret and 88 mm gun by hand desperately trying to line it up on the scout car. "I'll tell you when to go, then move like hell round the side of it" and he waited until the 88 mm gun was almost in line. "Now go go, go" and the scout car shot forward, accelerating all the time and passed the tank just before it was on target. Sergeant Jim knew it took two minutes to completely turn the turret and he knew he'd got thirty seconds before they were on target, then speeding round the tank he knew he'd got another sixty seconds before they could reline the gun and by that time he was out of sight and re-joining the squadron. But what a nerve, coolness to the extreme. It was dramatic listening to it unfold, as it happened but it must have been terrifically tense for him and his driver facing that tank and the feared 88 mm.

Helmstedt was a small town close to the main Autobahn that led to Berlin and it formed the barrier between the Allied Western Germany and the Russian Eastern Germany, and that barrier was manned by the Russians. When the war finished there was total distrust with the Russians and the Allies. There were even observation posts either side of the border each spying on the other. It was in this environment that fourth troop decided to make ourselves known to the Russians in a friendly gesture by going to see them at this control barrier. We pulled up in our vehicles and our officer got out and started to walk towards the building were the Russians were housed. Within a moment he was surrounded by Russian soldiers who virtually pushed him into the building. At the same time each of us was faced with a Russian, with a rifle touching our temple. At the end of the rifle was a pallid expressionless face, unblinking, stony eyes just looking down the sights, fingers curled round the trigger. For almost thirty minutes we were held in that situation, almost afraid to breath. Certainly, in my case avoiding the stare of the Russian that was threatening me. They released us as quick as they dealt with us originally.

Whilst I was in Helmstedt, following a meeting in the training classroom the Major decided that I must go on an instructor's course to Bovington near Bournemouth in England, for six weeks. When I returned the Sergeant Major had been demobbed and a Quarter Master had been made up into Sergeant Major in his place. In the interval several Sergeants had chummed up to him so that when I re-joined the unit, I was the odd one out and as "creeping" was not in my make-up there was a distinct coolness between us. It first of all appeared when on my return, as is usual, parades are shoved on to you and on the first guard parade which he attended (the reason was soon apparent) I assembled the guard in the same manner as it had been before I went away. However, I received a dressing down by the new Sergeant Major. (He'd altered it. New brush sweeps clean) I was told to use the official Army way, by calling out a marker, then right dressing them and so on. I was smarting and several Germans were about, looking on with interest. I knew he'd led me into it deliberately. So, I said in a stentorian voice "Right Sir. Get off my parade." (A little unusual but in fact the parade ground is always considered to belong to the one who's parade it is and I was the Duty Sergeant, so the parade was mine and that's how I treated it.) My order was loud and clear and before he realised it, he'd actually walked off and by doing so had lost the edge, but from then on I was marked man and for over two months I had to keep a step ahead of him all the time.

He was picking on everything and because I was Squadron Signals Sergeant and it meant I didn't do much in the way of parades or drills but he altered that and on this particular day he'd got me on dawn duty, followed by Orderly Sergeant and then listed me for taking a squad of freshly joined recruits in Drill scheduled for 9 a.m.

As I was up at dawn, I borrowed a scout car from fourth troop, my old compatriots, drove out some distance and disconnected the telephone line for the Squadron. (Now I'm telling secrets.) At 9. o' clock I was presenting myself for drill parade in best battledress when suddenly the Sergeant Major was called from the parade into the Squadron Office. Next minute he was out in double quick time addressing me. "The 'phones dead. Get out and find the fault." "But I'm on drill Sergeant Major." He retorted about the drill in naughty words and in effect said, "Forget the drill find the fault." I changed quickly then walked back along the lines pretending to examine it for faults and in due course reconnected the break, making sure that the drill parade had finished.

I was called into the office and thanked by the Major in the presence of the Sergeant Major, but the onslaught against me still continued until we moved.

It may be the reader is thinking "What a stupid act," disconnecting a telephone communications link, but let me assure you there was no risk. I knew that in the case of real risk or trouble, other lines of communication were open. I don't know exactly what they were, that was deliberate, it was only those who matter, who knew. We others should it be necessary would then be told and instructed. Additionally, I was more than aware, the German population in that part of the country, had, had enough and I found they easily complied with your wishes, though obviously there are always exceptions, but I still believe no risk was entailed.

When we moved, we moved in formation and I acted as Control for the move. I was in a large American Staghound Armoured Car.

Behind me was the Sergeant Major in a Humber Scout Car. He was known as *Dog 1* in radio procedure. Behind him was the Major, like me in a Staghound. We moved on and several messages were passed all going through me as Control, when suddenly the Major called up Dog 1. Now the Sergeant Major hadn't a clue about wireless procedure.

Until he was made up into Sergeant Major he was more used to issuing clothing and such like, so I was in the wonderful position, in the turret of the Staghound, of being able to look down on him and watch his face redden and begin to squirm as he didn't know what to do, or what was more important, what to say. I actually leaned over and gave him a smile. The Major repeated his call several times with more evident anger. As Control, I called up when I thought it had gone on long enough just before the Major had apoplexy and said to the Major, "It could be a microphone fault as I could see Dog 1 speaking but no sound was forthcoming." The following day the Major published orders that all ranks above Sergeant must attend wireless procedure cadres under the guidance of the Squadron Signals Officer and Signals Sergeant, (which was me.) Within minutes the Sergeant Major was in my classroom as nice as pie, treating me as though I was his long-lost friend. From that day the chasing stopped.

By this time the Squadron and Regiment was being affected by demobilisation and new intakes and it was decided that my Officer and myself would be transferred to Regimental Headquarters at Wolfenbüttel as Regimental Signals Officer and Sergeant. My Officer reported first, and I was to follow a few days later. A day or so after my Officer had moved, I was called into the Squadron Office and he was on the 'phone requesting me to bring his pistol and holster as he would need them for guard parade duties at the week-end. I collected them off his Batman and decided to go that evening by train from Helmstedt to Brunswick, then at Brunswick I could get an army vehicle lift into Wolfenbüttel. I buckled the belt with pistol, holster and bullet pouch around my waist and caught the train. Within minutes I thought it seemed to be travelling away from Helmstedt in the wrong direction towards the Russian Zone and the next stop could be Magdeburg and I knew if I finished up there, I would probably disappear. My train was travelling slowly doing about twenty miles per hour, so I jumped, plunging at least three feet to the ground managing to regain my footing, my legs buckling slightly but then regaining their strength, standing me in good stead as Uncle Bill once said and then continuing through the woods and intending to cross the Autobahn on my left, to return to Helmstedt. When I heard a woman's voice obviously in some kind of trouble. It was common knowledge that at night we would often hear the sound of rifle shots and occasionally spasmodic bursts of machine gun fire coming from the vicinity of the Helmstedt woods. Women were known to disappear, taken by Russian soldiers and we never seemed to hear of any results as to where they were or what had happened to them. All this was on my mind as well as the story of the treatment the young woman had told me in the Sergeants Mess at Wolfenbüttel. I moved forward quietly, and then I saw them. Five Russian soldiers with a girl held up against a tree. She was struggling and crying but she stood no chance. One was already stripped from the waist down. I was looking for the weapons, the guns they would have. They never leave a gun. I couldn't see any and was mystified. I thought afterwards they were probably under orders like we were, and they were out of bounds; the wrong side of the border and therefore wouldn't carry the weapons with them though most of them carried knives and there were five of them. More than enough to do what they wanted to do. I loaded the pistol but knew I couldn't do anything for fear of hitting the girl, so I decided to run out in an attempt to draw them away and sure enough they came at me, so I fired at them, hitting at least two of them. At this they changed direction and ran into the trees, one limping and one holding his shoulder.

I thought at first they were after their weapons. I grabbed the girl by the arm and shouted "Schnell, Schnell," practically the only

German words I knew which meant "Quick, Quick." We managed to get through the woods and back into Helmstedt. She took me to where she lived. It was an old people's bungalow and she and her mother shared one small room no bigger than a small bathroom. It contained a single bed in which both of them had to share with a space in front no more than two feet wide in which they had to do everything, cooking such as they could and whatever. Her mother had returned to their hometown, Kleve in the Rhineland for a few days. They'd been evacuated to Helmstedt due to the bombing. She was clinging to me and wanted me to stay with her, but I didn't. I put my fingers to my lips and said "Shush." Meaning the old people will hear you and I released her grip and left. A couple of nights later I was with a few lads in a hall where a dance was being held. I couldn't dance for toffee but at twenty or so what do you do? The girl was there and she made a beeline for me. We were married in March 1948 in St. James's Church, Wollaston, Stourbridge.

The Inns of Court Regiment was originally a cavalry regiment and was only formed in wartime, so now the war was over and demobilisation was taking place, it was in the process of being broken up and was in state of flux and those whose demobilisation wasn't imminent were gradually being transferred to other regiments that were being kept for occupation purposes. This meant that I would be eventually transferred to the 14th /21st Hussars based at Wuppertal in the Ruhr, the home of the Schwebebahn a single track overhead railway which followed the path of the river and actually travelled above it, all stations being built, raised high in the air, in order for you to catch the train. Some days before my move I was passing the rear of the Maintenance Sergeants base in which he carried out vehicle repairs and was also his accommodation. This sergeant was unknown to me having joined our regiment in the turmoil of other regiments being broken up. In the front of his workshop and billet there was a raised section of stone flooring about eight inches high and I was called, in German, by a civilian who was bending over a young woman in a bed made up on this raised floor surface. The civilian turned out to be a German doctor who was attending to the young woman who looked quite ill. The doctor asked me to hold her parted legs whilst he injected her with mercury-based fluid. I knew mercury wasn't good for a human being, but he convinced me there was no other option. Apparently, this woman had second degree syphilis and was the girlfriend of the maintenance sergeant, who agitatedly walked back and to constantly, looking pale and worried.

I sat on the floor facing the young woman's feet and gently placed my hands against her legs more for comfort and assurance rather than any attempt to hold them. When the doctor had finished and replaced the bedclothes over the young woman, I got up, turned and found the eyes of the young woman looking at me, they were sad, wistful, full of despair and sorrow but also with a look of gratitude, of thanks, for what little I'd done to help her.

I have carried that look in my memory ever since and have often thought was she by any chance saved or helped by the introduction of Penicillin which had arrived and was widely used very soon after, with results that were nothing short of miraculous, all venereal disease being cured in something like ten days. Had she have entered the third stage, medically known as General Paralysis of the Insane this would lead to facial bone structures collapsing as well as the invasion of the brain itself and nothing on earth would have saved her, also of course the treatment with mercury wouldn't have helped.

Before being demobilised all soldiers were given the opportunity of taking up a course to help them back into civilian life. I decided to study Accountancy and book-keeping and Government and Democracy and for this purpose went to Göttingen University in the Hartz Mountains. Unfortunately, I contracted a horrible fever with a vicious throat and could barely lift my head. I wore three or four shirts a day each time wringing them out like a flannel until finally I had to report sick. My throat was terrible and when the doctor examined me, he said, "I think you've got Diphtheria" and he injected me with the serum. I felt it draw my eyes together as it took effect and he sat by my bedside until 9 o' clock at night, when the ambulance came and took me to Hanover hospital. I was examined by a lady army doctor who took a swab and felt my glands and I didn't hear any more for three days until she came and said, "It's Glandular Fever the symptoms of which are identical to Diphtheria." By the time I felt better, it was time to return to my unit without having undergone the pre-release courses.

The Adjutant, called me into his office and asked me if I could formulate fighting units and crews in the regiment for the next three months taking into account the rate of demobilisation and the trades people concerned. I said I could, providing I could have a list of all personnel, their trades and their demobilisation dates. From this I was able to do the job. Apparently, he was praised for the accuracy of it after a few weeks had elapsed and the accuracy of it was proven. From this I was given a pile of demob booklets which every soldier was given and contained a character reference that I was asked to write. These references were in respect of Regimental Head Quarters. Squadron, ninety odd men in all, embracing cooks, batmen, store men and all the echelon people. In fact, I hardly knew any of them as I'd been in A Squadron with a fighting troop so I made it my business to see everyone involved and spoke to them, learning something about them and from this sketchy information I compiled the references which the commanding officer signed prior to that individual being demobbed.

Then when the regiment was being broke up, I was transferred to the 14th / 21st Hussars stationed at Wuppertal in the Ruhr. Once again, I contracted Glandular Fever which apparently comes in waves and can return more than once. Again, I was treated for Diphtheria necessitating lying flat on my back in bed for six weeks and during this time the Adjutant in this new regiment called and tried to entice me to sign on for several years' service. I didn't but he did get six months out of me.

All the men in the ward were in a similar position to me which necessitated lying as still as possible in bed. This often meant for long periods there was silence, when in all probability a lot of thinking was done. In order to break this silence, I often told stories of memorandum or of films etc and one evening as the light was darkening, I began telling of the story of the film "*13 Rue De Madeleine.*" A film starring James Cagney as an F.B.I. Agent.

At a moment in the dark, the patients in the ward breathlessly waiting for the climax of the film when one of the patients in the end bed, a guardsman, who had been extolling the virtues and praise of the story suddenly yelps and shouts for the nurse and no one is present, we hadn't seen one for ages. His cries became more urgent until eventually. "Nurse, Nurse I'm dying." At 11 o'clock a nurse turned up. The guardsman who thought he was dying, rigor mortis, his whole body stiffening was proven to be O.K. He was allergic to Penicillin, which was very new, we were amongst the first to receive it and side effects were not yet known, though notes and observations were being kept.

It was at this hospital where the same Guardsman had seen large carboys of orange liquid stored in the passage by the bathrooms and one night requested a drink of the orange pop which he'd seen there. The nurse promptly said he could have one if he wanted but it wasn't pop it was urine. Apparently, it was stored before being sent to the local German hospital for them to distil it to extract the penicillin from it. That same hospital today is from all accounts one of the leading hospitals in Europe. How times change.

I visited Krupp's at Essen, occupying seven and a half square miles. During the war employing seventy-five thousand workers many of them slave workers, all being capable of being evacuated to bomb shelters under the factory reinforced floor within two minutes. We were guided by one of the Krupp's family, a distant cousin who spoke good English and could not have been considered to be a war criminal otherwise he wouldn't have been allowed to do the job he was doing. One shed was that large; when we stood at one end, we could see a white area in the distance the size of a postage stamp. This in fact was the opening at the other end of the same shed. Inside, almost lost, were a couple of trains which looked like miniatures. In another building there was a huge press, the largest in Europe it was said, if not in the world. Above, it appeared to be a little hook which we were told actually weighed ten tons. We travelled around the area in a jeep. It was far too large to walk. At one stage I noticed a huge barrel of a gun lying at the side of the road. On enquiring Herr Krupp said with a wry grin it was intended for a new super Tiger Tank but after it was made, they discovered that the tank would be too large and heavy for any road or bridge in Europe. "We all make 'em" he said, meaning mistakes. It was a touch of humour I saw in Germany and refreshing at that.

I was demobilised in September 1947 and because my mother had moved to Stourbridge to be with my dad this was now my new home and I must admit I didn't like it as much as Llandudno. On my way home I had to report to a demobilisation Depot in York where I was issued with a civilian suit manufactured by Burton's. I had been away from home for something like four and a half years and in that time my mother had only received a weekly allowance of ten shillings a week so I was determined to buy her something and I bought a bottle of sherry and placed it in my small pack which I carried over my shoulder. On stepping into the train in York to travel to Birmingham, I slung the small pack onto my shoulder and in doing so the bottle of sherry slipped out of the pack and smashed, disappearing into the station platform. I watched in horror as it dissipated through the tarmac surface and my heart sank. It seemed like the end of the world. I'd bought it deliberately as a little gift from the heart, for a mother who had had an enduring hard life, receiving very little and it hurt me deeply when I had to tell her when I got home, but she dismissed it as an accident and nothing to worry about which was like my mother all over.

Chapter 3

Back Home

My first job was trying to pick up the threads of Accountancy and Auditing with a West Bromwich firm of Chartered Accountants. I didn't like it that much maybe it was because most of them were more knowledgeable about the business than I was.

Having just finished four and a half years in the army and as young as I was, I was very conscious and curious of religions. During my quest I visited many types of churches and meeting halls relevant to most of the everyday religions, embracing Catholic, Jewish, Christadelphian, Baptist and so on and finally visiting a Spiritualist church probably because my mother was interested in it and spoke favourably of it saying that she'd never heard addresses that could compare with what some ordinary person of no particular prestige could give in clairvoyance. But she always added that should you receive a message from a medium you should never help them in any way by giving them facts or information they can build on. The best way is to answer yes or no whenever possible.

After attending a séance that was given by a Bristol medium which was exacting in many details with no help from myself I was travelling back from an Audit in Bilston and had arrived at Brettel Lane station with Dennis my great friend from the accountancy firm who I'd discussed the clairvoyance with, one part of which I couldn't understand and which the medium had said in no uncertain matter, "You will." But crossing the railway bridge at Brettel Lane it suddenly hit me from nowhere and stopped me in my tracks. Dennis meanwhile was running over the bridge because he had seen two buses approaching one going in his direction, the other in mine and he shouted this to me, but I was so struck once again by the accuracy of the message which previously I'd been unable to understand. The result, Dennis caught his bus, but I missed mine.

The next day I was telling him and one or two other employees of about it and as it was in the week that Christmas Day fell in, with not much work being done on the last day. It was decided, not by me, but by general vote to hold a séance in the office using a large round table for that purpose. Alphabetical letters were cut out, laid in a circle with a half pint tumbler inverted with each of the staff resting a finger on the glass. I was initially elected to ask the questions which I did. At first the response was hesitant then a little quicker, spelling out the answers and words by moving from one letter to another. By now a partner in the business was an onlooker, slightly apprehensive and looking rather pale Some of the assembly were now accusing each other especially me of moving the glass, which I certainly wasn't. A question was asked, frivolous and nonsensical and the glass started racing around the letters. Dennis was copying the letters down as fast as he could write, trying to decipher them. At the same time as he cried out "Crikey. It's said bugger off the lot of you." the table reared up about twelve inches off the floor to the exclamations of everyone. The Partner fled from the room. I didn't see him again until some weeks after Christmas, but nothing was spoken of about the incident. When I told my mother what had happened she said "Well, like draws like and you were acting the fool so drew a like for like response."

I later joined W.J. Brookes as an Office Supervisor. This was without doubt the happiest job I've ever had. My work consisted of running the office, banking, paying of accounts, wages, cashing in the van salesmen, recipe costing etc. I also started a social club, three pence a week from all members, occasional pub do's and at Christmas a wonderful Christmas dinner with entertainment and dancing involved to which non-members were invited which brought in girl and boy friends, husbands and wives. Wonderful times.

In March 1948 I married Gerda. Gerda on her father's side was from a strong Roman Catholic family, one or two being priests but it never created any trouble for us. There were difficulties, however. People on both sides had lost loved ones. My mother had lost a son. Gerda's mother also her only son. Gerda a fiancée, a sub-mariner an awful wartime occupation and at the war's end that awful realisation and knowledge of the concentration camps, Belsen, Auschwitz, Buchenwald and so on all weighing heavily on our population and on our minds.

To my abject disbelief and shame, I cannot even remember asking my parents if we could live with them, but they never raised any objection and made her welcome. It speaks richly of the value of parents and that knowledge which often comes too late in life.

I can't criticize Gerda she was spotlessly clean in every way. She tried her best to cook in the English style, she liked to shop, to buy new clothes etc and I did my best for her, but money wasn't too plentiful. After some months she felt homesick and I could understand. She was taken away from her homeland and her mother who had no dependants. Her mother's husband who had something to do with the film industry had left her some years before. I managed to pay for Gerda to go home for a month. She returned and we continued our life together but in due course she wanted to go home again but instead we brought her mother over, for her to see what her daughter's life was like here. Her mother enjoyed the visit especially when we saw "*Singing in the Rain.*" Knowledge of the language was hardly needed for that. Her mother went back and Gerda after some months once again visited her homeland. This time she stayed a while longer and I managed (though currency restrictions were difficult and costly) to supply her with a weekly amount of cash to help her out. It began to feel as though I had brought a plant from some foreign country and the roots were just failing to grow and the plant was wilting and dying. She came back and there was some disagreement because she wanted a place of our own which I understood and couldn't argue with but in those days, council house waiting lists in Stourbridge and Dudley were up to nine years and because I hadn't put our names on the list she was annoyed.

Once again, she went home and whilst she was away, my parents who rented a house were offered it as sitting tenants at a price of £850, by a Jewish owner, it was said he owned fifty or sixty houses around the Midlands. He wanted to sell all his holdings so that he could emigrate to the new settlement in Israel. The £850 meant there was no deposit, no legal charges and all road charges were thrown in.

My Father

My father said to me "We're too old now but you can do it. It will give you both a foot on the ladder." I wrote to Gerda, but she never gave an answer and when she returned, she was annoyed because I'd gone ahead with it. I'd done so because I was faced with a deadline and I had asked her, but she didn't reply. Also, if I hadn't have done it, the house would have been sold to someone else and then no one in the family would have had anywhere to live.

In no time at all she was back in Germany and it is to my continuous regret that I couldn't transmit money to her, to help her, as being my wife that was something I was conscious of and concerned about and wanted to do. In retrospect I feel a certain guilt especially for that and for knowing it's not easy for any couple starting out in married life under the same roof as your parents. Although they were never any trouble to us in any way, it is an absolute necessity to have your own privacy, especially I feel, for the woman. Today when things have changed considerably that may not be so important, but it certainly was then.

Also, in retrospect the circumstances that caused us to meet were exceptional and may have contained a certain "knight in shining armour" context to it and the gratitude that Gerda must have felt at that time. Also, we were both young. I was no older than twenty-one and Gerda was younger, and I was totally inexperienced where women were concerned, and I can only hope that Gerda and her new family found a life of happiness and contentment back in the country of her birth. I am saying no more on this matter because I can hardly be critical and have no reason to be, especially when she is not here to defend herself.

Chapter 4

Husband, Father and Widower

One day a new girl started, in W.J. Brookes, tall, blonde, long legs like a thoroughbred, twenty-two years of age, hair cascading to her shoulders. Eight stone, vivacious, lively, happy go lucky, tremendously quick in everything she did. The fastest comptometer operator I've ever seen, her name was Freda. We often worked close together and I was soon conscious of her feelings towards me. She never probed or inquired into my circumstances though I think she knew. Always I was aware of her presence and how much she was beginning to mean to me, then one day when Gerda was in Germany, the last time she visited there and which became permanent I received a letter, she asked me for a geschieden - a divorce. Anyway, nothing could be started for three years and then it took ages. It wasn't until the thirteenth of June 1959 that Freda and I could be married. In that summer my father and mother died within twelve days of each other never being able to see the grand children that followed. Although my mother who was poorly at the time didn't know Freda very well, my father did. Freda had got him to lay some lino in her mother's flat and to make some curtains and she cooked him a dinner which he never failed to talk about. He rapidly thought the world of her so that was two of us.

For seven or eight years whilst the separation and divorce were going through, we wrote to each other every day despite the fact we saw each other with almost the same frequency. After we were married Freda brought so many shoe boxes all filled on end with the letters we had written to each other. They were burnt in the garden. As there were so many it was impossible to keep them and as Freda said, "We have no further need for letters" and she added. "We have each other."

In my recollections and deliberations, I have thought at oft times of the great love stories in fact or fiction, but none of these so far as I know were in limbo for seven or eight years. The wasted years, wonderful young years for having children and they were lost to Freda, yet in all that time when her brother was forging ahead to become what I have heard said was the largest producer of three-piece suites in Europe. Freda was hostessing no end of parties, business meetings, functions, shows and so on, meeting Company Directors, Chairmen, Accountants, Solicitors etc; many of whom propositioned her, and never once did she listen, falter or encourage. To the reader this may represent dreams or fantasy; to me it is and was reality.

After we were married, I too used to attend many of these functions and although I couldn't dance for toffee, Freda was the opposite. A most wonderful natural dancer who looked so much at ease on the dance floor that everyone wanted to dance with her. Not only that, but she would play her part whether they were good dancers or not. It was a fact that whoever she was with was enhanced purely because of her, but always at the end, no matter who she was dancing with, she would excuse herself, walk over to me and "drag" me on the floor for *"Who's taking you home tonight."* She was also a good storyteller with a touch of the comedienne. She could even tell a risqué joke so beautifully; it was never offensive, rude or crude, never shocking, producing gales of laughter. No wonder the men were like flies around a jam pot and despite all this she favoured me. Wasn't I lucky?

The magic of being in love - very little money - but loads of love. Our trips together. Day trips to London, fourteen shillings return on a football special arranged for the Arsenal West Bromwich game but we were visiting the London Palladium to see Danny Kaye at his best, when he held the audience in the palm of his hand and another time visiting the Lyric Theatre in Hammersmith to see Emlyn Williams in his solo role as Charles Dickens and the beginning when he walked from the wings in evening dress complete with beard, the spit of Dickens, approaching the rostrum in deathly silence, peeling off his white gloves, still with the sound of silence. A packed theatre - every seat occupied, people standing all around the theatre, leaning against walls that had chalked on it, ten standing here, five here and so on, all round the theatre. The only space, the centre aisle, left open on the Watch Committees orders in case of evacuation, fire etc. Then the train back home. Not allowed on until 11.58 pm; arriving in Dudley at 3 o'clock in the morning, then the walk home with Freda and my own walk from Dudley to Stourbridge about 5 to 7 miles. Phew! The power of love and I'd do it all over again. Cinema visits, back row customers, perhaps some sort of skimpy meal beforehand if we could afford it. The walks, miles and miles out into the country, our lives welded together undoubtedly the greatest times of our lives. All surreptitious trips.

Before we were married during those seven or eight years our relationship was secret. We used to meet in all sorts of places, air raid shelters, parks, pubs, empty buildings, and her brother's van anything and everywhere.

One time when we were entering a derelict building in Dudley and it was Winter, freezing cold and I'll always remember, I don't know how it came about but she said "I have never been afraid to go anywhere with you and I never will." I didn't ask for it, but it was nice to hear.   We walked gingerly into the empty factory building. It was pitch black and we suddenly dropped through a hole in the floor, the height of the drop being the height of the room below. We hit the floor and as we fell, I held her to me and lifted her so that she fell lightly. I was O.K; once again my legs had stood me in good stead (Uncle Bill's words) but I laughed, we both did as she said with her lovely candour. "I think my knickers are around my neck."

Another time in Haden Hill Park in Old Hill we were desperately looking for somewhere to go. We made our way to the Park buildings and we both climbed through a window finding a bench seat inside. Heaven! We'd been there for some time when a torch beam was aimed through the window we'd climbed through and a tremulous voice said "Right! You in there come out. I know you're in there." Fortunately, the only light was the policeman's torch, so he was unable to see my face or Freda's as we both clambered out through the window. The policeman took our names and addresses, but we didn't hear any more about it.

We used to travel some Saturdays to Worcester by train. Walking from Shrub Hill Station into Worcester town, past the cricket ground out into the country, eventually leaving the road and crossing the fields and we'd have a picnic on the banks of the Severn. The picnic was an art in itself. Everything being prepared by Freda the night before. The salad contained in crumbled ice in plastic bags to keep fresh and the sandwiches airtight in a sealed container. On one occasion returning to the roadway to make our way home, it was necessary to mount a steep bank to get on the road and as we were struggling up the bank, Freda slid over the edge a drop of about four feet and landed only twelve inches away from spiked railings in a mass of stinging nettles. She managed to get up by pulling on my outstretched hands. Her legs were one mass of rising lumps from the stings. I left her whilst she removed her tights and returned with loads of dock leaves which she wrapped around her legs before replacing the tights to hold them in place. When we got to Shrub Hill station, I bought her a brandy (for the shock) which she wasn't too keen on. She said next day that she hadn't slept a wink that night for the throbbing and the heat generated by the stings.

One time we stayed for a week in Conway, North Wales and another time in Llandudno where I showed Freda all the places I'd known and loved and once we had a week in the Isle of Man, staying in Castletown. The lady who originally was going to put us up was taken ill and she gave us another address, which turned out to be the premises of a grocer's shop, the old type, wooden floor with sawdust on it and hams hanging around. Our rooms were on the upstairs floor of what was previously a warehouse for the shop below and the grocer man had created rooms by using partitions which in height finished about two feet short of the ceiling and he'd used all sorts of materials for the construction. My bedroom door quivered when you closed it. But everything was spotlessly clean, and the woman fed us as though she was fattening turkeys for Christmas. We called it the *"House that Jack built."* It was on this holiday that we had a marvellous bus journey from Castletown to Ramsey at the other end of the island. We sat upstairs at the front so that we had a good view of everywhere we were going. At the back there was a family of three or four children with their mum and dad and they provided a wonderful show of singing in harmony, in pairs and solo. They were brilliant and Freda spoke of it for years afterwards.

It was in 1959, that wonderful summer, Saturday 13th June when Freda (pictured on next page) and I were married. I was working at Old Park Engineering at the time. The wedding took place in Stourbridge Registry Office. My greatest regret that it wasn't in church, but Freda never minded. I always felt that I should ask Freda's mother for her daughter's hand in marriage. Freda's father had died some time before, but I met him a few days before he died. He took my hand weakly and looked into my face and said, "It's been a nice day today hasn't it?"

I nodded clasped his hands and bid farewell, knowing as I looked into his eyes how poorly he was. He died two days later. My own parents died also during that summer within twelve days of one another.

So, there was the mother. Although I was uncomfortable about being divorced, I was not afraid to ask her for her daughter's hand, but I was afraid of looking into her eyes and perhaps seeing dismay or disappointment at her daughter's choice. This was something I didn't want to see. It may not have happened, but I didn't want to risk it. I don't think it would have happened from what Freda said. Her mother was only happy that Freda had made her choice. Freda knew and understood my reticence and she said lightly, "Oh don't worry I'll tell mother" and so she did, and everything was lovely.

Three or four years after we were married we went to Dublin on holiday, whilst we were in Ireland we went for a trip to somewhere or other and there was some kind of large granite obelisk and legend said that if you could put your arms around it and your fingers touched you would be granted whatever you wish. Out of all the party on the coach, Freda's was the only one whose fingertips touched. Shortly after we returned home, she discovered she was pregnant with Glen and it was then she told me that is what she had wished for.

She had hypertension during pregnancy, huge sickness each night lasting two or three hours, with never a moan and she was taken to the Women's Hospital in Wolverhampton two or three weeks before time. During the pregnancy her strongest liking was for peaches. She must have eaten dozens.

I visited the hospital and saw that tiny bundle of flesh, not wrinkled, but sun kissed with a light tan (must have been the peaches) helpless, dependent entirely on the mother. I marvelled at this greatest miracle, the beginning of life and the love of the mother, the strongest love in the world and ever since I've seen nothing to change my mind. Women, mother's especially. They are wonderful that's why I love them. We were overjoyed when Melanie arrived later. What a darling she was. As a baby she would be outside in the garden, in the pram fast asleep, but when she awakened, she would start doing acrobats, hanging upside down from the pram in her harness trying to touch the floor or the wheels of the pram or something. Memories, that I will always cherish.

Me with Melanie and Glen

Glen

A son of immense stature, of integrity, honesty, ability and determination. Glen as a young lad, quiet, studious and extremely intelligent. He excelled at everything. Never a need to "Crack a Whip." Certainly, a touch wilful as a teenager (but who isn't at that age?) Never a need to worry about drink or drugs or spending money that he didn't possess. There was never troubles of that nature.

Reams could be written about Glen, but it would be more worthy and interesting if he wrote his own memoirs embracing his life, skills, ability, forward thinking and achievements. They are so numerous they'd fill more than a book, monumental. As a son he has provided me and his mother with so many reasons for pride and assurance that he is one of those son's any parent would give their life for. That is enough. Glen must write his own life story that will be something.

This is a bit of a postscript, written many months later, actually January 2017 when a day or so ago Glen was on the 'phone and mentioned that he was purchasing a Fibulator for the village of Tettenhall, in memory of his mother. I was that pleased and Melanie too when I told her. As a father I feel I understand that sons are not quite so "touchy feely" as daughters are. They tend to keep their feelings quiet, inside them, but nevertheless such actions as those described, emerge at times and you are made aware of feelings that were kept, intact, secure and in secret and it's wonderful to know.

Melanie

A daughter of worth, of quality, memorable as a child for hanging upside down out of her pram, supported by straps, steam and the overpowering smell of ammonia rising from her nappy, but feeling, searching looking for adventure and then wreathed in smiles as she was rescued from that position by her wonderful mother who fussed and changed her in a second. Her constant falling over when if she moved anywhere, it was always done at a gallop, rather than walking, resulting in damaged and grazed knees, knocking her head on head height furniture when rushing by, resulting in father fixing polyether sponge on each of the offending pieces of furniture at head height.

Today as always, she is the essence of goodness, thinking very much like her mother, of others more than herself. Comfortable, again like her mother with what she's got and in no way desirous of wealth in any quantity but is happy so long as she can get by.

Other qualities or talents, in brief are her brilliant organising abilities. I would have no qualms of putting her in charge of any operation, function or celebration, knowing full well it would be dealt with effortlessly, right down to the smallest detail, and another facet, like her mother, her speed of thinking, her immediate response to a request, an enquiry, and an expressed thought. Done more often than not before you can think about it and as an adult what a beauty- caring, generous, good-hearted, happy go lucky, but still quite vulnerable, but a jewel of a daughter who enhances my life each and every day and I know for sure embellishes others too.

I cannot possibly talk about Melanie and Glen without referring to their other halves, Tony and Zoe. Obviously, I can't talk about them with the same depth as I can of my own, but let me just say, we are, I believe all content with one another. There have never been any disagreements, upsets, aggression or unhappiness. These are all worthy qualities and valued and I feel well pleased and extremely blessed with what I and they have got.

Freda

I would think in these memoirs Freda's name will appear more than once. It's bound to. She was the greater part of me and my life and therefore it's necessary for her to be spoken of in the same context as myself. She was born in Cradley Heath, Graingers Lane, to be exact on the 21st of June 1928. She, her mother, father, brothers Percy, Cliff and Gerald lived in this small terraced house sharing a communal  back yard and I believe an outside toilet with a number of other houses in the attachment. Father worked in the coal mines, Percy too, until he was involved in a pit accident which severely injured his leg and which after several operations necessitated amputation. Money was scarce and life itself was very hard, but they lived like many others at the time by wearing hand-me down clothes and going without.

The great thing about this living was that it led you to understand what life was about and stood you in better understanding of poverty and want when poverty was a real name, poverty when you had no soles in your shoes, replaced by cardboard, no seat in your pants, replaced with a patch, no food in your belly, replaced by hunger, the memory of it remains with you the whole of your life and provides you with knowledge that no riches or education can give.

Freda was the embodiment of this. She was always content with what she'd got. She never had desires for riches or wealth, never any animosity or jealousy towards others who had it. She would remark whenever this was raised in conversation. "I have everything I want. I only need enough to get by," and so often she would be looking at me as she said it. I was always conscious of this love that flowed from her. It was never shown by constantly holding hands or names like darling or honey, but by actions, gestures and the warmth that exuded from her. Her qualities were endless. I never remember missing a meal in my life. She'd come in from work, coat still on and in a very short time we'd be eating. She also cared for her mother until she passed away at the age of ninety-one, finding her four houses, one after the other, purely by her own efforts and persistence. First in Wordsley, then in Quarry Bank, then in Stafford and finally in Haughton. Despite work and the family, she would take her mother a hot meal every day and sit with her in her latter days often doing the laundry whilst in her company. She was the most wonderful daughter a mother could ever have, wife too, though she always had some sort of guilt complex that she had never done enough. What a falsehood. She was more than golden, she was an angel right down here amongst us, and that realisation is even more recognised now than it ever was when she was here with us.

She thought of everyone. I remember for years she used to buy over thirty Christmas presents for members of the family all of which was saved out of her meagre allowance from her weekly wage. This fortunately was reduced as the children reached adulthood but even then, she wrote and sent cards to all and sundry. I still follow this pattern today, walking in her footsteps. I feel it's my duty as well as an honour and a tribute and even a debt which I can never fully repay.

Since I have lost Freda, I have felt at times hopelessly lost, hollow, empty, and bereft. Initially there was shock wrapped up in grief, but on reflection, shock being the greater of the two, then came the grief, emphasized by everything I did, especially knowing that Freda had done it before, and it was all mine now. This weighed heavily upon me and I was saturated with despondency. Outwardly bright. I could laugh with people, talk with them but always my mind was elsewhere and inwardly I was hurting. My only salvation was our children, Glen and Melanie and I knew I had to hold together for their sakes and their other married halves. I've found different people are a help, undoubtedly my own family connections, but others too.

I have to go out just to get out. I look for company in the throngs in the supermarkets. People around me seem to help. I need to talk, and I can't talk enough. I feel I've got to find some solution before it's too late. It was at this time of utter depression when I went on holiday to Seven Oaks in Kent and I met the three ladies mentioned in the preface to these memoirs and who proved at that time to be lifesaving.

Outside I can talk, laugh, joke but inside is undiluted misery. If it wasn't for family, life would be joyless, not worth a cent.

Norman Williams World War 2

Postscript

In June 2019, Norman was invited to join 300 former service men and women celebrating the D-Day landings. In typical Norman fashion here follows his written account of the 7 days and nights he spent as a guest of the British Legion.

These are the feelings of one man who was lucky enough to be invited by the Royal British Legion to go on the D-Day 75th anniversary cruise, for seven days finishing up at Normandy

The activities, events, memorial services. Everything exacting perfection. Nothing could be bettered and all the prominent people that were present, became almost one of us, one of the crowd. Talking to everyone and anyone. No 'side'. Often embracing, shaking hands, making a fuss. Even kissing individuals, or rather individuals kissing them, including Mrs May!

From the word go, everything was done for us. Carrying the luggage, helping us up the gangway. For those in need, wheelchairs were provided along with someone to push them.

Nothing quite like it has been done before and it is unlikely to be done again. The cost to the Royal British Legion is reputed to be well over a million pounds.

We weren't looked after - we were nursed. Completely spoilt. So many people on our side, breath-taking, difficult to digest. Now back to reality, home, but with memories that will remain with us for the rest of our lives.

Unforgettable.

This is my record of the 75th D-Day anniversary trip to Normandy.

Sunday 2nd June 2019, Day 1 – Dover

We were taken from home to Dover arriving there after a 7 hour coach trip to be met with the band and escorted through 2 lanes of naval and service lines who saluted us as we walked between them into a vast receiving hall full of tableclothed tables and being served with tea, coffee, and cakes while being entertained by 2 lady singers in WAAF uniforms.

After this we were led into the ship after being helped, where necessary, up the gangplank by members of the military forces which were there in abundance waiting on us - some pushing the more troubled of us in wheelchairs. On entering the ship, we were issued with a tape to hang around our neck with every detail on it about us. This had to be shown and slipped into some little gadget that checked us out as being genuine - the security was intense. We were handed a shopping bag containing an umbrella and a pin badge and later, after a glorious meal, we were entertained by the 40 odd members of the Royal British Legion band with Rod Stewart present singing appropriately enough "Sailing". his wife, Penny was walking around talking to everyone she met, and they were queuing up!

Monday 3rd June 2019, Day 2 – Dunkirk

Town visit. Presently surprised no damage from the war. Lovely old buildings. At night we had the showgirls entertaining us with dancing thrown in, supported by a 7 or 8 piece band . Both permanent fixtures of the Fred Olsen shipping line.

Tuesday 4th June 2019, Day 3 – Poole

Today there was a visit into Poole for those who wanted it. I stayed on board to listen to a lecture by Peter Snow, a great talker who mixed with the audience afterwards answering any questions they posed.

The Royal British Legion band was playing almost all the time. In the evening there was showtime entertainment with AJ off 'Strictly Come Dancing' who again mixed with the audience afterwards and this was followed by a magician who was also very funny. Lance Corporal Jones (I think his name was) a winner of 'Britain's Got Talent'. Later, I met and talked with an elderly mischievous lady. full of vigour.r who is possibly the last of the code Breakers who were at Bletchley Park.

Wednesday 5thJune 2019, Day 4 – Portsmouth

This was a huge occasion - police and army everywhere dozens and dozens of them - security so intense due to the presence of the Queen, President Trump and Mrs May and many other political figures all saying their own words on the occasion. Commented by Celia Imrie songs by Sheridan Smith, brilliant march past, must have been several thousand people present. Afterwards a packed lunch in a huge marquee attended to by members of the armed forces.

Charles and Camilla walked around mixing and speaking with all and sundry, Sheridan Smith also outside in the crowds again going out of her way to speak to people. In the evening, we watched the flotilla that accompanied us as we left for Le Havre with the Red Arrows flying overhead and two warships passing us with all hands lining the deck from stem to stern with their hats symmetrical against their bodies along the whole line - a truly impressive sight! We also saw Don Snow filming for the BBC "One show".

Thursday 6th June 2019, - Day 5. – Bayeux Cemetery, Le Harvre

Today we had a huge outdoor service with what must have been at least five thousand people. Security at its highest due to the Prime Minister and other prominent people being there as well as Prince Charles and Camilla. I've got a feeling Prince Charles and Camilla won over many, many people today for they walked amongst everyone talking with ease throughout. This was afterwards, in the large marquee, where we had a reception. Again, we were waited on by army personnel being entertained as we ate by an opera singer – lovely! The Royal British Legion band were accompanying her.

Friday 7th June 2019, Day 6 – Le Havre

Today the weather was not so good it was raining when we visited Pegasus bridge, Free drinks were supplied in that cafe that was first liberated and then onto Arromanches. Because of a driving error (due to poor sat-nav instructions), we arrived late only allowing us 45 minutes but time enough for a huge fuss to be made of us with presentations of €100 in vouchers which had to be spent in Arromanches plus a backpack, a hat, a poncho, and a medallion.

A band was present on all these occasions. We were led to any shop we choose to spend our vouchers. I received 2 bottles of whiskey one bottle of calvados and 2 tins of sweets all under the guidance of a lady who orchestrated the way in which the vouchers could be spent remembering that time was at a premium. In the evening, the D-Day Darlings took the stage with the band always at hand. The D-Day Darlings were the 6 young ladies who dressed as WAAFs and won the 'Britain's Got Talent' competition last year. After the show, they mixed with everyone posing with photographs with anyone that asked including me (who didn't ask).

The overnight return to Portsmouth was cancelled due to the high winds and rough sea.

Saturday 8th June2019, Day 7 On Board.

As we sailed back to Dover being entertained constantly by the Royal British Legion band the conductor captain Cole being honoured with an OBE by the Queen and announced on this very day.

In the early evening, a cocktail party followed by the gala dinner and afterwards a concert with the D-Day Darlings and the showgirls. We were also addressed by Bob Gamble, head of the Royal British Legion, who thanked us for being there – (fancy thanking us?) A superb finish to a week that all will remember for the remainder of their lives. Oh, and I nearly forgot, on arriving at Dover we were welcomed by a drummer band on the quayside

Sunday 9th June 2019, Day 8. Homeward bound

Eight-hour coach journey back to living an ordinary life!

End note

You will notice, I have composed these words, not as written but as if I'm talking to you, the reader, that's the way I like to do it.

I had already word-processed up today 7 and then I pressed the 'save' button but when it printed I lost everything except day 7 so I had to do it all again which might explain any sort of mess-up in the composition… this old age is no good!

26870940R00088

Printed in Great Britain
by Amazon